# THE BIG
# LONG

**www.amplifypublishing.com**

*The Big Long:*
*How Going Big on an Outrageous Idea Transformed the Real Estate Industry*

**For more information, please contact:**
Amplify Publishing, an imprint of Mascot Books
620 Herndon Parkway, Suite 320
Herndon, VA 20170
info@amplifypublishing.com

Library of Congress Control Number: 2021915208
CPSIA Code: PRV1121A
ISBN-13: 978-1-64307-552-5

Printed in the United States

To our parents, who encouraged us to take
chances and make mistakes.

COLIN
WIEL  DOUG
BRIEN

# THE BIG
# LONG

## How Going Big
## on an Outrageous Idea
## Transformed the
## Real Estate Industry

amplify

# Contents

# Introduction

*Now, one thing I tell everyone is, learn about real estate. Repeat after me: real estate provides the highest returns, the greatest values and the least risk.*
—Armstrong Williams, entrepreneur

It was early 2012. We had just closed a $200 million round of capital investment for our company, Waypoint Homes, and were in high-octane growth mode. After an unnerving but exciting beginning, when we could scarcely believe we were the only people who had perceived the opportunity amid the wreckage of the 2008 San Francisco Bay Area real estate market, we had turned our business model into a thriving company with thousands of homes in our portfolio, nearly two hundred full-time employees, and several hundred high-net-worth investors.

However, we were also adrenaline junkies. We had locked Waypoint into an exhausting pattern. We would burn through our capital buying home after home until we had only a few months of cash left to keep the lights on and pay our people, like two guys joyriding in a Corvette and headed for a thousand-foot cliff we could see in the distance. More than once we had come to the edge of disaster only to reach out to our network of high-net-worth investors to raise funds just in time to keep us alive—the entrepreneurial equivalent of twisting the wheel, slamming on the brakes, and skidding in a cloud of dust to a heart-stopping halt inches from the edge of a drop-off like something from a Road Runner cartoon.

Think *Thelma & Louise*, only with two guys: a former NFL football player and a UC Berkeley engineer. And while we didn't actually drive off the cliff, we came very close to catastrophe more than once. Then, in 2011 and 2012, our push to grow Waypoint as aggressively as possible took us right to the edge of the abyss. We were down to a few weeks' worth of cash in the bank, with a critical financing deal that had appeared to be a sure thing suddenly unraveling before our eyes in less than twenty-four hours.

Oh, by the way, that was all happening while we were being investigated by the FBI for possible violations of antitrust law and living with the threat of being sent to federal prison! Other than that, 2011 and 2012 were pretty boring.

But if you're really going to appreciate our story and what we did with Waypoint (and our new company, Mynd), we first need to take you to early 2021 and a merry band of outlaw traders on Reddit.

## GameStop and "Big Short" Thinking

You probably remember that back in January and February of 2021, a populist uprising of Reddit stock traders drove the price of flailing shopping mall video game retailer GameStop into the stratosphere and stuck it to a bunch of hedge fund investors to the tune of billions of dollars. Quite a victory for the little guy over the Wall Street billionaires, right?

Not so much. There was a little bit of David-beats-Goliath, but mostly what played out with Reddit, Robinhood, GameStop, and the cofounder of Chewy.com and hedge fund giant BlackRock was a cynical, misunderstood example of the scorched-earth investment strategy known as "going short." As you might have guessed from the title of this book, we approach business and finance from the opposite perspective. Here, we'd like to demonstrate why.

You probably know the basics of the story. A Reddit investing group called WallStreetBets, whose members had a penchant for messing with short sellers, found out that some major hedge funds were "shorting" GameStop stock and decided to buy the stock and artificially drive up the price to hurt what they saw as greedy hedge fund billionaires.

"Going short" means you're betting the price of a stock will drop. You profit off that bet by borrowing shares of that stock from someone who owns them, selling the stock, and buying the shares back at a later date to return them to the party you borrowed them from. The short seller bets that after he sells the stock, it will go down in price. Then he can buy the shares back at that lower price and return them to the lender, keeping the difference as profit. Short sellers get in trouble when the price of the stock goes *up*. They're obligated to buy the stock back at that higher price and can lose a fortune. That's called a "short squeeze."

That's what happened to some of the hedge funds that owned GameStop. Reddit's activities put the short squeeze on some big Wall Street players. But while some WallStreetBets members made a nice profit and a few hedge funds like Melvin Capital and Citron took a beating, the harm to small investors was actually a lot greater, while the rich got richer. Trading app Robinhood and other brokerage services suspended trading of GameStop after a six-day GameStop buying binge, bringing a halt to all other trading on those platforms and wiping out an estimated $11 billion in value. And while BlackRock and Chewy.com cofounder Ryan Cohen made a fortune, plenty of starry-eyed, inexperienced day traders who bought the "meme stock" lost their shirts when the bubble burst.

In other words, the GameStop saga represents capitalism at its worst—cynical, voracious, and willing to manipulate markets for short-term profit with zero concern for the long-term effects. That's the "going short" mindset that made pop culture heroes out of the people featured in best-selling author Michael Lewis's 2011 book *The Big Short: Inside the Doomsday Machine*. If you haven't read the book, there's a good chance you've seen the Oscar-winning 2015 film of the same name starring Christian Bale and Steve Carrell.

Both the book and the film chronicle the run-up to the 2008 real estate meltdown that crashed the world economy and the handful of savvy investors who saw the disaster coming and took advantage of their foreknowledge to make billions. The "big short" Lewis referred to in his book was the bet by a small number of investors and others that the US mortgage-backed security market, the largest asset class on the planet, was headed for an unprecedented collapse when millions of over-leveraged borrowers began defaulting on their mortgages en masse.

Popular culture, and especially the movie version of *The Big Short*, have turned the investors who made billions by betting against the housing market into folk heroes, crusaders making the big banks pay for the corruption, greed, and stupidity. But they are no more Robin Hood than the GameStop traders who thought they were sticking it to The Man. "Big short" thinking profits off carnage and misfortune, produces nothing, and leaves devastation in its wake. It's why the average person hates Wall Street.

We believe capitalism can be more than that. We believe entrepreneurs have a responsibility to build for tomorrow, not just take profits today and head for the hills while regular people deal with the damage. Instead of the big short, we've developed a philosophy we call the "big long." In the financial world, "going long" on an investment means buying an asset with the expectation that it will increase in value over time. In our world, it means thinking big and building something with an eye on creating value for the long term—not just for ourselves, but for shareholders, employees, customers, and the community.

In going for the big long, we thought big and long term from the start, investing our time, effort, and money to create something meaningful, something that would transform the real estate industry, create a new asset class, and even help people who lost their homes to the Great Recession find a path back to homeownership. That's capitalism at its best: creative, productive, and serving people—not just generating profit. That's the guiding star we tried to follow. After you read our story, you can decide for yourself whether we are succeeding.

## Swim or Die

Since 2009 we'd adhered to our philosophy of "going long" in growing Waypoint Homes, a "buy-and-hold" investor in the single-family rental (SFR) market. Our business model was straightforward: we had developed a proprietary technology platform that helped us locate undervalued single-family homes in real estate markets hit hard by the 2008 foreclosure crisis and then acquired, renovated, rented, and managed them with the same kind of technology-driven efficiency. Our portfolio of rental homes yielded both healthy year-over-year cash flow and long-term asset appreciation while giving renters a path back to owning homes again. It was the polar opposite of the GameStop episode— creative, productive, and a terrific business model that no one thought possible.

However, Waypoint was like a shark. Sharks have to swim constantly to keep water and oxygen moving over their gills; if they stop swimming, they asphyxiate. Our company's growth and continued survival depended on our ability to continuously locate, make offers on, and acquire new single-family homes. Naturally, that takes a great deal of capital. We needed sufficient cash to make offers on thousands of homes each month and close on hundreds of them. That's what it took to keep our pipeline full, keep us growing, and satisfy our obligations to our investors.

When Waypoint was smaller, we simply borrowed against our portfolio and used that capital to buy more properties. That had gotten us through our early life, but our growth needs quickly outgrew that funding source. We moved to raising private funds from wealthy individuals who sought long-term profits from the SFR market. By 2012, we had raised three funds that were performing very well. But now even that well of capital was beginning to run dry. To scale Waypoint to a size that would enable us to reach our goals—and to put us in a position to survive inevitable competition from rivals with virtually limitless resources—we needed to do something different: borrow money from a big bank.

Our plan was to raise $200 million from a private equity firm, secure another $400 million in debt, buy $600 million worth of houses, and invest in developing an even more robust technology platform that would enable us to manage our portfolio with optimal efficiency—in effect, to transform SFR from an impossible-to-manage curiosity that left most investors spooked into a bona fide asset class. That would also give us the operating capital to keep the doors open and continue paying our employees.

In December 2011, we locked up the private equity half of the deal with GI Partners and went bank shopping. The good news was that lots of banks were interested. Waypoint was growing quickly, and while we weren't the only player in the market anymore, we had a big head start over well-funded latecomers who were beginning to notice the SFR opportunity but had not yet pulled out their checkbooks.

Nobody had ever tried to structure a debt deal like this for an asset class like ours. We were seeking a single loan that would be secured by a large pool of houses, many of which had not yet been acquired. Technically, we were getting the loan to buy the collateral for the loan—the financial equivalent of pulling yourself up by your own bootstraps. Our business model was too unnerving for some banks. But then we found our bank: Wells Fargo. Much, much more on them later.

Wells Fargo liked our track record and thought our growth model was sound, and we settled into a six-month process of putting together an unprecedented deal. During the negotiations, we also realized that a tremendous irony was playing out. If we closed the deal, Wells Fargo would be lending us money on some of the same properties they had lost when the real estate market collapsed. Like most banks, they had taken massive losses on subprime loan defaults, so they were understandably cautious about our deal and spent months gathering as much information as possible. It's bad enough to be burned once, but no one wants it to happen a second time.

Meanwhile, Waypoint was rapidly burning through the $200 million from GI Partners by continuing to buy hundreds of homes a month. But even though we were down to perhaps three weeks' worth of cash (a refrain that would repeat many times during Waypoint's existence), as the summer 2012 closing date for the deal approached, we were confident. Excited, even. Soon, we could leave behind the endless cycle of calling investors and raising funds!

Remember that old line about best-laid plans?

Without warning, the bottom fell out of our deal. We've had a running joke for years that a crisis always occurs when at least one of us is on summer vacation. That summer, Doug was in Cape Cod and Colin was in Lake Tahoe when we got the call. Days before our loan was scheduled to close, one of Wells Fargo's highest-ranking executives saw the deal . . . *for the first time.* We're not sure how that happened, but we know what happened next. He killed the deal. With the stroke of a pen, our loan was dead. So, possibly, was Waypoint.

So much for vacation plans. This was a five-alarm fire. We raced back to San Francisco and began putting together emergency plans that would let us keep Waypoint's doors open while we searched for new funding options. One option was to lay off 70 percent of our employees but keep a small satellite operation alive to manage our existing SFR portfolio. If we did that, rent would keep coming in and our homes would appreciate, but buying new inventory would be out of the question. Our economics in the GI Partners deal would also be at risk because our fee hurdles were predicated on securing debt. Without debt, we would never hit our goals and earn our promoted interest.

We also hated the idea of letting any of our people go. We had built a tight-knit team over the past four years, one that grew in a high-intensity, perform-or-perish kind of environment that created a bond among its survivors—a bond that still exists today.

## Citibank to the Rescue

So, before taking any drastic measures, we decided to see if we could find another bank that would do our debt deal. At the same time, we did something we had hoped we'd never have to do again: raise another fund. We had already met with Citibank, and we circled back to them to see if they would work with us. At the same time, we called every investor on our list. Knowing that we were at risk of going to this particular well once too often, we worked hard to create an impression of scarcity that would make investing more enticing.

We told our network of high-net-worth individuals that this would be our last noninstitutional deal ever. "Get in now, while you can" was the pitch. Thank God it worked. Over two exhausting, stressful weeks of twelve-hour days during what was supposed to be our summer vacation—keep in mind, this was happening *while* we were being investigated by the FBI—we raised $30 million. That was fund number four.

We had a bridge that would keep us alive while we closed institutional funding. The trouble was, we were burning so much cash buying homes that the $30 million only gave us two months of life. We had to close our deal with Citibank, and we had to do it while keeping the whole affair quiet. If we didn't, our employees might panic and start looking for new jobs. We needed them to remain focused on their work: making offers, overseeing renovations, and managing our properties. So we put on our calm faces while Doug ran the company, Colin took the lead on property acquisitions, and our third managing director, Gary Beasley, dealt with Citibank.

Citibank became our knight in shining armor. We closed the deal in just six weeks. On October 3, 2012, a story came out in the *Wall Street Journal*: Waypoint Real Estate Group had closed $245 million in loans from Citigroup. It was the first large-pooled debt facility for SFR in history. We would live to fight another day.

Ironically, Wells Fargo, which hung us out to dry by pulling out of our debt deal at the eleventh hour and fifty-ninth minute, later became a business partner and an investor in our follow-up company, Mynd. But that's a story for later in the book.

## Going Big When Everyone Is Thinking Small

When all this financial drama occurred, Waypoint was still one of the only small, individual partnerships to enjoy large-scale, lasting success in the SFR industry. All our later competitors were huge corporations with the ability to raise and spend massive amounts of capital: Blackstone, the biggest owner of real estate on the planet; Colony American Homes; Starwood; and American Homes 4 Rent. We were there before any of them.

However, when we launched Waypoint in 2009, nobody really wanted anything to do with the SFR market. It was considered too chaotic, too widely dispersed, and too fractious. Rather than investing in a few large buildings containing hundreds of residential units, SFR meant buying and managing individual residences that might be distributed over thousands of square miles. With no single point of contact and hundreds or thousands of individual tenants to deal with, investors regarded SFR as akin to herding feral cats. It wasn't until mid-2011, after we built the technology infrastructure the sector had always lacked and created a scalable, growing operation, that large institutional investors roared into the space and began throwing huge amounts of money at the SFR market.

If you'll pardon us for taking a brief victory lap, Waypoint was the first company to establish SFR as a legitimate, mainstream investment opportunity and attract institutional capital. We probably weren't the first entrepreneurs to imagine SFR as something more than the purview of "buy-and-flip" investors, but we were the first to look at the map of scattered, independent properties with no central hub for underwriting, renter acquisition, communications, or maintenance and say, "Hey, what if we *became* the hub?"

In other words, when most everyone else was thinking small about SFR, we had the nerve to think big and go long. That's the story we want to tell in this book—not that we're smarter than everybody else or more visionary, but that by thinking big and going long when nearly everyone else around you is thinking small or chasing short-term profit, you can build something extraordinary that helps people and even changes an industry.

There were other talented, bold entrepreneurs out there trying to build scalable platforms. We may have raised the first institutional capital and led the way in terms of building out industry-changing technology, but these companies were legitimate pioneers too. The Treehouse team from Phoenix, led by Dallas Tanner, ended up selling to Blackstone and becoming Invitation Homes, where Dallas serves as CEO today. Former hedge fund manager Aaron Edelheit started the American Home and did a great job of building that company up until he sold it to Silver Bay. American Residential Properties was another outstanding early company, led by Steve Schmitz and Laurie Hawks. They did a great job of building up a portfolio in the Phoenix area that was later acquired by American Homes 4 Rent.

## The Opportunity Everyone Saw but No One Saw

No one could have predicted the growth of SFR as an asset class when the world seemed to be ending back in 2008. The real estate market had collapsed, the economy was in free-fall, and it looked like we were headed into a second Great Depression. In 2008, Silicon Valley real estate prices fell to their lowest point since 2002; it was the area's worst year for home sales in decades. People everywhere were losing their jobs, the stock market was plummeting, and homeowners in blue-collar East Bay cities like Pittsburg, Richmond, and Vallejo were getting crushed by falling home values, job losses, and foreclosures.

According to the *San Francisco Chronicle*, of the more than twelve thousand Bay Area homes that went into foreclosure in the third quarter of 2008—an increase of 273 percent over 2007— 6,183 were in Alameda and Contra Costa Counties, and most of those were in the poorest communities. By the time the carnage was over, housing prices nationwide had dropped 23 percent, and homes in East Bay cities like Antioch and Richmond had lost up to 70 percent of their value. This was a human tragedy because families were winding up on the street.

During that dark time, we were both fortunate enough to be financially secure, with the luxury of looking for new investment opportunities. However, practically everyone in Silicon Valley and the real estate investor community had dismissed the idea of pursuing single-family rentals. The conventional wisdom was that the inventory was too decentralized, dealing with tenants was too time consuming and expensive, and getting to scale would take too much cash. Given the undercurrent of fear and panic that was everywhere, it seemed safer to stick with multifamily or commercial real estate.

However, we saw something nobody else was able or willing to see. Perhaps we were ignorant or stubborn, but whatever the reason, we didn't dismiss the idea of SFR as a business model out of hand. Instead, we said, "Let's not settle for assumptions, anecdotes, and conventional wisdom. Let's gather the data and see what they say." We figured if the data told us that the conventional wisdom was right and SFR really was a quagmire, we would lose nothing but a little time.

When we looked at the data, we saw a market with extraordinary profit and growth potential sitting there in plain sight, with no one taking advantage. Our willingness to take a closer look at the math and the trends behind the Bay Area housing crisis, not to mention the increasing power and availability of mobile and cloud computing and big data, became an opportunity that changed our lives and transformed the real estate industry.

## Big Long Thinking

Why were we the ones to do this? Why not more experienced real estate investors? Why not one of the giant REITs? In part, it was because of "big long" thinking. When we did a deep dive into the numbers behind the Bay Area SFR market, we saw that while home prices had fallen off a cliff, rents had remained relatively stable. We could've said, "Cool, let's buy four houses, fix them up, and flip them." That's what most investors at the time were doing—thinking small and short term. Instead, we thought big. When we looked at the numbers, the desirability of the Bay Area, the number of foreclosed homes, and the area's relatively solid job market, we immediately scaled up our idea of what was possible. Rather than think in terms of four houses, we thought in terms of four hundred and then four thousand.

The key to Waypoint's origin story is that from the beginning, we thought big and went long on our idea. We began as a small company, because all start-ups do. But from day one, our goal was to acquire as many properties as possible that fit our financial model. We went long for several important reasons:

1.  We trusted our data. While other investors were avoiding the SFR market based on gut instinct mixed with fear of the unknown, we believed our hard numbers. Numbers don't lie.
2.  Our confidence that Bay Area real estate market valuations would rebound.
3.  The once-in-a-lifetime prospect of being first in a potentially enormous and untapped market.
4.  The chance to define a new industry.
5.  The opportunity to help people and rebuild communities gutted by the crisis.

**6.** The inevitability that, sooner or later, the big, private equity firms would get wind of the opportunity in SFR and quickly swoop in. We wanted to be big and established before that happened.

Big long thinking is the success secret we want to share with you. Going long on your ideas when everyone else is counseling caution comes with risks, but it also has the potential to pay off in ways that short-sale thinking cannot. How do you know when you're approaching a business opportunity or investment in this way? First, you're probably one of the few people (maybe the only person) who sees the opportunity for what it is; everyone else is stuck in their own bias or fear. You're probably the first mover, or one of the first movers, in the vertical. You probably have a body of data proving that the opportunity is real, which we did. Our data was so compelling we could scarcely believe no one else was doing what we were doing.

But maybe the signal trait of big long thinking is that you're thinking big from the outset. Your year-one goal isn't to move into an office with six employees and fund yourself with a home equity line of credit. It's to land a $5 million seed round of funding on your way to a $30 million C round as you grow fast and grab market share before anyone else knows what's happening. Sounds fun, right? It was.

## How We Did What We Did

We're going to share with you the thought processes, strategies, and tricks that enabled us to turn the "impossible" SFR market into a pioneering real estate investment trust (REIT) that had more than six hundred employees, owned more than seventeen thousand homes, and ended up merging with some of the largest players in the SFR market.

So what's the secret? There is no single secret. We set out to build something based on the principle that renters are also hardworking people who deserve care and respect, and we did that. We set out to assemble a team of terrific people who would play hard, have fun, and care about each other, and we did that. We set out to show real estate investors that with technology, SFR could become a legitimate asset class worth taking seriously, and we did that.

If there is a secret sauce, it's that from the outset, we thought big and went long, with the intent of building something meaningful and sustainable. We had some nerve-racking moments, but we never doubted that we were right. We're going to share the inside story of Waypoint—the good decisions and the dangerous ones, the near-disasters and the big wins, and the people who made it possible.

Did our hyperaggressive, throw-caution-to-the-wind approach lead to some harrowing, bizarre, hilarious, and sometimes frightening occurrences? Of course it did. We've already mentioned being investigated by the FBI, a time of stress and apprehension that lasted for about two-and-a-half years. There were the seven CFOs we hired. We found naked drug dealers sprinting out of our houses. There was the time we saw somebody murdered, and the pre-IPO investor tour where we were so punch-drunk that we couldn't stop laughing. There were the countless times we were a few weeks away from running out of money. None of which should be surprising, since neither of us had ever done anything remotely like Waypoint before! We were making it up as we went along.

There were also the renters who cried and hugged us when they found out they could stay in their homes, the contractor tenants whose work was so good we hired them, and the early employees who are still like family to this day. You'll meet some of them. We'll talk about how everything we learned at Waypoint led us to launch our next venture, a property management technology company called Mynd, and some of the crazy events surrounding that launch, including how we attempted a Series C fundraise in the middle of a pandemic and stock market collapse and got more than one hundred "No" answers, until we finally closed the round with fewer than sixty days of cash on hand.

It's been quite a ride.

We're going to tell our story from a "we" point of view, like we're both sitting on a couch across from you, walking you through everything that happened. From time to time, we'll talk about ourselves individually (i.e., "Doug did this," "Colin said that," and so on). When we do, just imagine that one of us is giving you the scoop on the other.

Why go to the trouble to write and publish a book? Because we want to share what we learned about SFR and tell our story. We believe in the power of both helping people achieve great things and improving the world for everyone. We want you to have access to that power too. We also believe in giving back, and as fortunate as we have been, it's time for us to do that. As you read, we hope you will be entertained, learn more about real estate, and take away any lessons about business, finance, technology, and entrepreneurship that will help you meet your own goals. We hope you'll embrace the mindset of going long.

Let's do this.

**Doug Brien & Colin Wiel**
San Francisco, California

# CHAPTER ONE

# Swim Against the Current

In 2008, Warren Buffett gave an interview to Charlie Rose where he said, "You want to be greedy when others are fearful. You want to be fearful when others are greedy." The word *greedy* isn't appealing, but the Oracle of Omaha's message is correct: *when everyone else is going in one direction, don't be afraid to go in the opposite direction.* However, that is easier said than done.

For example, today there are many young and ambitious companies transforming sectors of the real estate industry with technology. On June 21, 2019, *Fortune* ran a feature called "Meet the A.I. Landlord That's Building a Single-Family-Home Empire" about Amherst Holdings, a real estate investment firm that currently owns about 16,000 SFR, using artificial intelligence to identify SFRs in the Rust Belt with the highest potential to generate short-term cash flow and long-term appreciation.

Then there was a piece in the *Wall Street Journal* from June 19, 2019, titled "The Future of Housing Rises in Phoenix" about how companies like Zillow, Opendoor, and Offerpad were using algorithms to find and grab premium buy-and-flip properties in the Phoenix area, one of the markets hardest hit by the financial crisis. These companies are doing innovative things and creating extraordinary value.

However, it's one thing to go long in a proven market or to rely on technology that's already been tested. It's another to be one of the first to put your resources and reputation on the line to find out if that market exists at all or to create the essential technology from scratch. That's what we did. We'll go into greater detail on this later, but by 2010, following Colin's lead, we had developed a sophisticated system to leverage live data feeds that weren't available a few years earlier. When a house came onto the MLS in any of our markets across the country, we had immediate access to property, school, and crime data, and within an hour, our intelligent algorithm told us the maximum price we should pay for that house. SFR wasn't scalable until Waypoint used technology to *make* it scalable.

Being ahead of the crowd means there is no one to warn you when you're about to make expensive mistakes. Banks and investors steer clear of you. That's what we experienced. While most everyone was reeling and fearful from the real estate collapse and some investors were looking for Bay Area buy-and-flip opportunities, we looked at the shattered remains of America's housing market and thought we saw a new industry: large-scale SFR ownership and management driven by data and technology.

## The Cal Berkeley Connection

Being an entrepreneur is incredibly hard, and we all have blind spots. Both of us had strong skill sets in business and technology, but separately, we would not have made Waypoint work. We needed each other. When we started talking about our ideas for the SFR market, we realized that our talents and passions complemented one another's perfectly.

Our backgrounds were very different. Doug was a soccer player and a football walk-on at Cal Berkeley who earned a football scholarship in his sophomore year and ended up starting for three years. He became a placekicker, set the school's all-time scoring record, and ended up getting drafted in the third round of the 1994 NFL draft by the San Francisco 49ers. In his first year in the league, he won a Super Bowl ring.

But Doug didn't want to be one of those guys who played in the league for a few years and ended up with nothing to show for it. So with $200,000 in his pocket after his rookie year, he started studying real estate and realized that it was a great asset class where you could grow value with renovations and create not only long-term capital appreciation over time but tax-efficient current income. "My goal was to play in the NFL long enough to save enough that I could do what I wanted to do instead of what I had to do," he says.

In the 1995 off-season, after winning the Super Bowl, Doug bought a run-down house in Oakland, and he and a friend did the renovations themselves. During the next off-season, he became part of a syndicate buying an apartment complex with a family friend, and after that he decided he would make one real estate investment every year during his NFL career. He had also received an NCAA postgraduate scholarship, so when he signed a five-year contract with the New Orleans Saints, he used that scholarship to enroll in the MBA program at Tulane University, studying real estate finance. Being a placekicker who wasn't required to attend as many meetings as the other players, Doug would spend his off-hours reading finance books in the training room, much to his coaches' chagrin.

"I was getting my MBA at Tulane while playing for the Saints," Doug says. "As a kicker, you can only attend so many meetings. You can only lift so much weight. I'd be at the training facility with all this time to myself, so I'd pull out a finance book and be sitting in the training room reading it. Jim Haslett was our new head coach, and he used to come by and be like, 'What are you doing?' He thought it was the funniest thing.

"What I heard was that Coach Haslett came to the conclusion that school and business were more important to me than kicking, and so even though I ended up kicking 80 percent that year—and averaging more than 85 percent over my prior five years on the Saints—they let me go at the end of the year," Doug continues. "I remember thinking, *Maybe I shouldn't have been studying real estate finance in the locker room, and maybe I should stop thinking about and studying business and do it for myself.*"

By the time he completed a twelve-year career (the average NFL career lasts just over three years), Doug had his MBA and had learned to love finding undervalued assets, doing his due diligence, adding value to them, and creating compelling cash flow. When he retired from the NFL at age thirty-five, he had enough money to do what he wanted, his real estate license, and enough knowledge not to be dissuaded by conventional thinking.

While he also attended Cal Berkeley, Colin had a different experience. He was a mechanical engineer interested in robotics and automatic control systems. After graduating, he went to work for Boeing writing algorithms for controlling aircraft systems using artificial intelligence. During his four years at Boeing, he invented a new way to control antilock brakes. After leaving Boeing, he became an independent consultant and software engineer and spent a year consulting at Netscape during the early days of the internet, becoming one of the first Java programmers.

Java became the language of e-commerce, and Colin ended up developing a curriculum for UC Berkeley Extension. He taught evening classes in Java programming to engineers, building a network of his best and brightest students. Many of them became his employees in 1998 when he started his first company, Milo, a software engineering consulting firm doing e-commerce infrastructure. The dot-com boom was in full swing, and everybody wanted to get into e-commerce, so Milo was in high demand. The company grew as fast as Colin could hire more people, and among its accomplishments was building Charles Schwab's online trading website, the largest e-commerce website in the world at the time.

Colin sold that company in 2000 (just as the dot-com bubble was starting to burst) and began investing in real estate. In 2004, he and a friend went fifty-fifty on two mobile home parks and then bought a ministorage facility. They sold those properties after three or four years, but by that time, Colin was hooked on real estate. While with Boeing, he had also started trading in the stock market using a long-term buy-and-hold strategy. "My strategy was to just buy Microsoft stock, and that's the only stock I owned," he says. "As I saved more money, I just bought more Microsoft stock, and that stock went up one hundred times. Then in 1992, I sold half my Microsoft and bought AOL, and that stock went up over one hundred times. So I'd only ever bought two stocks, and they both went up one hundred times. Then I did the same with Yahoo, and that went up one hundred times."

We shared that same investing mindset. We liked defying conventional wisdom. We liked finding the cases where we were able to see investment opportunities other people missed. And we both loved the potential of real estate as an asset class. That's where our paths crossed.

## The Bomb

It was late 2008, and we knew each other because we were both part of the same Bay Area angel investor group, the Keiretsu Forum. Every so often, this group of entrepreneurs and investors would get together to talk about ideas and opportunities. One day the topic was real estate. The real estate collapse was in full swing, and as unnerving and horrible as it was, entrepreneurs know that opportunity is always hiding in disruptive change if you can set aside your emotions enough to see it. We were there to discuss strategies, brainstorm, and see if any possible investments stood out.

Coincidentally, both of us had been looking with interest at the situation with single-family homes in the East Bay. If you don't know the San Francisco Bay Area, there is a lot more to it than San Francisco itself, tech-rich areas like San Jose and Silicon Valley, and wealthy enclaves like Palo Alto and Sausalito. There's also the East Bay, which is home to blue-collar cities like Pittsburg, Antioch, Concord, and Vallejo, working-class enclaves with a lot of minority residents. They are exactly the kind of markets that unscrupulous lenders targeted with risky subprime, adjustable-rate mortgages in the years leading up to the financial crisis.

Those subprime loans were one of the leading causes of the real estate collapse. As Michael Lewis chronicled in *The Big Short*, for several years in the early 2000s, mortgage lenders started writing loans for people who didn't qualify for the more common (and more secure) thirty-year fixed-rate mortgage. Maybe they didn't make enough money, maybe their credit scores were too low, it doesn't matter. Instead of saying no to all that business, lenders offered those buyers—many of them working-class families—riskier adjustable-rate mortgages, or ARMs, with low "teaser" interest rates that would reset to much higher rates after maybe three or five years. Eager to buy homes in a national market where real estate prices were skyrocketing, people ignored the future rate hikes and signed on the dotted line. As long as housing prices kept rising, they would be able to refinance, so everything would be fine.

Meanwhile, those higher-risk mortgages were bundled into mortgage-backed securities. Banks sold trillions of dollars' worth of those bonds to institutional investors—state pension funds, university endowments, and so on—all over the country. By the mid-2000s, the entire economy was a bomb, with tens of millions of bad mortgages as the ammonium nitrate and millions of over-leveraged investors playing the part of the fertilizer. The only thing keeping the whole thing from going off was the idea that home prices would somehow go up...*forever*.

Starting in 2006 and 2007, the teaser rates on those ARMs began to expire, and the interest rates shot up. The bomb detonated. Some homeowners' monthly mortgage payments doubled and even tripled. Defaults and foreclosures skyrocketed. The housing market collapsed. Mortgage-backed securities went to zero, banks failed, layoffs began, and in 2008, the worldwide carnage we all know about started in earnest.

## Single-Family Rentals:
## Unmanageable or Misunderstood?

While all this was happening, we both noticed that although home values were plummeting nationwide, rents in the East Bay did not come down at all. How was that possible? Well, compared to the rest of the country, the Bay Area job market was still fairly strong, and even after being foreclosed upon, people still needed places where they could live and commute to work. They had simply gone from being homeowners to being renters. This math—a drop in home prices of as much as 70 percent but stable rents—was *very* interesting.

At our investing group meeting, everybody was talking about their favorite strategies—office buildings near freeways, shopping malls in tertiary markets, and the like—and then Doug spoke up about how much he loved the idea of buying single-family rentals in the East Bay. Dead silence. It was as though we had just suggested buying Lehman Brothers stock or investing in dial-up modems. The other investors in the group hated the idea and told us why in no uncertain terms. Then Colin shared the same interest. The room exploded with disbelief. We had lost the respect of all these people . . . until we got it back.

Why the animosity toward single-family rentals? Because conventional wisdom at the time said that single-family rentals were nothing but headaches. If you own a portfolio of properties scattered around a geographic area, they are more difficult, and therefore more expensive, than apartments to maintain. Instead of managing single buildings that can be overseen by single superintendents leading a small staff, you're dealing with hundreds or thousands of individual homes with roofs, yards, and fences that might need repair—not to mention hundreds or thousands of independent renters with their own needs and demands. The operational complexity of handling maintenance calls for a widely distributed portfolio of properties could wipe out your cash flow all by itself.

At the time, large investors had scaled rentals into a profitable asset class primarily by buying large buildings. That let them apply a formula. For example, for every one hundred units it owned, a company might hire an on-site staff of three people. Simple and predictable, which is just how investors like it. Nobody had a model for making SFR work at scale. Nobody even wanted to hear about it. They just dismissed the idea.

But we disagreed, and after that fateful angel investor meeting, we got together and compared notes. We looked at the data, and apart from the distressing numbers about home values and fore-closures, something else stood out. This was the Bay Area. Land is always at a premium, even in a faltering economy, and that's especially true in a densely populated area like San Francisco and its suburbs. With prices having fallen 50, 60, even 70 percent, no one would be building new housing inventory, even in the East Bay, until sale prices could exceed construction cost plus a profit margin. That wasn't likely to happen for years. With the cost of construction and the difficulties posed by factors like municipal zoning requirements, the obstacles to building were becoming more difficult to surmount.

The bottom line: in working-class communities, demand for single-family homes was likely to exceed supply for a long time. That meant there might be an opportunity, perhaps an unprecedented one.

We also saw that we shared the same conservative investing philosophy when it came to real estate: *buy and hold*. Find a great asset, buy it, add value up front through renovations, and get the cash flow from rent while it appreciates. It's a phenomenal investment model, and the potential for appreciation in the Bay Area, where normally sky-high property values were at their lowest point in decades, would never be better.

We decided the conventional wisdom might be wrong. The allegedly impossible might be possible. Everyone in the real estate world was running away from SFR, and we realized that this was the perfect time to see if swimming against the current was good advice. Was investor apprehension about single-family rentals based on facts or fear? We decided to find out.

## Thinking Big from the Beginning

Here we come to the first important aspect of big long thinking: *start out thinking big.* Yes, we were just beginning our investigations, but our intention was to figure out if there was the potential for something larger than the typical buy-and-flip investing or building a small portfolio of rentals. We had our eyes on something bigger, even though at that point we had no idea precisely what it was.

It had also become clear to us that we complemented one another well. When one of us was stumped for a solution to a problem, the other usually had an idea. It's become a cliché that entrepreneurs travel in pairs, and there's a reason for that. Building a business in any field is incredibly complex and demanding, and no one person, no matter how bright or educated, can know or see everything. So it's essential to partner with one or more people who are strong and experienced in areas where you're weak.

As we grew Waypoint, we discovered that there were some

natural differences between us that served us well. Colin is a technology visionary and innovator. Doug is a razor-sharp real estate mind and highly skilled at working with people and handling the day-to-day demands of driving a company. So while we both did everything, we quickly learned that things ran smoothest when we stayed in our lanes. Doug focused on hiring, running Waypoint, and running down properties for our portfolio. Colin built out the technical infrastructure that powered our entire business model. It was a natural, effortless dynamic.

That's why from the beginning we decided we would always be fifty-fifty partners. Since those early days, we have always had great chemistry: we hang out together, vacation together, and genuinely enjoy each other's company. We have always been identical in our power over the company and our economic interests, and that gave our work a spirit and energy that was nothing but positive. Sink or swim, we really were in this together.

## Opportunity on the BART Line

After that angel group meeting, a quick lunch revealed that we shared the same thinking about single-family rentals: there seemed to be an opportunity. But was it real or wishful thinking? We decided to do our due diligence. We would study the housing market and the data. Our operative question became, "What are we missing?" With that, we started driving around East Bay neighborhoods to assess their desirability, the condition of the homes, and what it might cost to renovate them.

The cities of the East Bay—cities like Martinez (population 35,000), Vallejo (population 116,000), Pittsburg (population 63,000), and Antioch (population 112,000)—have little in common with Bay Area stereotypes. You don't see dot-com millionaires, the creative class, flawless Victorian homes, and all the other things commonly associated with the Bay Area. Those communities are humbler and simpler, home to working folks whose families often go back many generations to immigrants who came to California from Mexico, Central America, the Philippines, or Africa. We drove through their neighborhoods keenly aware that we were looking at people's homes, not just buildings.

Whenever there is a rash of foreclosures, as in 2008 and 2009, the condition of the housing inventory becomes a big issue. People forced out of a home because of foreclosure are often angry, and sometimes they will vandalize the house on their way out the door. In a survey from 2008 by Campbell Communications, a research firm based in Washington, DC, realtors estimated that about 50 percent of foreclosed properties had suffered intentional damage by the former owners, from stripped-out appliances and holes in walls to pets locked inside to urinate and defecate everywhere. The problem is so common that it's routine for banks to offer to pay the former owners if they vacate without trashing the place.

We walked through houses where the owners had poured concrete down all the drains, knocked holes in the walls with sledgehammers, and even written obscene messages on the walls in human feces. Even if the former owners had not wrecked the property, most of the houses we saw had been sitting vacant for months. Peeling paint, waist-high grass, mold, and rodent infestation were not uncommon. Meanwhile, we were doing our best to underwrite our construction costs—to estimate what it would cost us to bring each house back to rentable condition and how much rent we could charge.

From the beginning, we focused our attention on neighborhoods along the Bay Area Rapid Transit (BART) line. BART is the region's light-rail system, and its different branches run through most of the communities we were planning to target. Our intention was to buy homes in the nicer neighborhoods of these lower-cost communities, because while you pay more, you get better long-term appreciation. We were betting on the resilience of the Bay Area economy and people's need to get to work.

Even with the national economy in tatters, the Bay Area was still a desirable place. We had Cal Berkeley, Stanford, and other University of California and Cal State campuses giving us a highly educated workforce. Silicon Valley was still the center of the tech universe, with superstar companies like Apple, Facebook, and Google. On top of that, we had all the food and culture and natural beauty of the region. We figured if any part of the country could weather the economic disaster, it would be the Bay Area. That meant there would still be jobs and people who needed places to live that were near those jobs.

Because of BART, the economics looked good. BART made it practical for working-class folks to live farther from San Francisco, Oakland, and San Jose, where the jobs were located. Even if you had lost your house, you still had to get to work, and BART was a simple, low-cost way to get around. We hypothesized that houses along the line would remain attractive to renters and hold their value. Plus, as far as we knew, nobody else was using this metric to look for real estate investments. The coming months would prove if we were right or wrong.

## CHAPTER TWO

# Believe the Data

A few months later, after looking at hundreds of vacant houses ranging from pristine to hopelessly vandalized and gathering lots of data, we had built our business model. Our data came from a variety of sources:

- **The Multiple Listing Service (MLS).** The MLS gave us data points like historical pricing data and comparable prices for houses that had sold since the real estate collapse. Comps were especially valuable because they gave us a baseline to work from in determining what kinds of offers to make.
- **Historical rent data for neighborhoods.** You can use public databases like Zillow or the Census Bureau's American Community Survey or private sources like Apartments.com and Axiometrics to get average rents by the year for zip codes or

even individual neighborhoods. Realtors and brokers also helped us determine rental prices. This told us how stable the rents were in the areas we were looking in and whether the rents we needed to charge were sustainable.

- **Renovation prices from contractors.** This was easy because as we went around to homes and met with realtors, we also met contractors and construction laborers who were eager to work. Construction of new homes and renovation work on existing homes had come to a nearly complete stop, leaving contractors, carpenters, electricians, and other tradespeople eager to give us sweetheart deals on everything from framing and tile to plumbing and electrical. It looked like we would be able to affordably renovate the houses we wanted to buy.

By the end of 2008, we had a treasure trove of data about home values, East Bay rents, neighborhoods, renovation costs, foreclosure rates, average rents, carrying costs, and loan terms from banks. We had a plan, but now we had to test it in the real world. Mike Tyson once said, "Everybody has a plan until they get punched in the mouth." We had developed our hypothesis over lunch in a data vacuum, but now we had real numbers on real properties, and it looked like our idea was going to survive. In theory, we should have been able to purchase homes in desirable East Bay neighborhoods for well below their previous market value, renovate them at a very reasonable cost, and then lease them for rents that would produce attractive returns.

Now it was divide-and-conquer time. Doug scouted for properties we could purchase. Colin started talking to the banks. With information in hand, we began making low-ball offers on vacant single-family homes. Our rationale was that the banks that now owned these foreclosed-upon properties would rather sell them to us than warehouse them on their books. We were pretty confident this was a tremendous opportunity—not just because the numbers were so compelling, but because as far as we could tell, no one else in the region was doing what we were doing.

This is another part of the big long approach. Remember, you will probably be out on a limb with your idea, just as Dr. Michael Burry and his fellow short-sellers were in *The Big Short*. A lot of people will tell you you're crazy, and overwhelming conventional wisdom might have you thinking they're right. However, to go big on an idea, there comes a point where you have to trust your data and your gut instincts and make the leap.

Frankly, while this can be an exhilarating time, it can also be terrifying. No matter how good the numbers look, no matter how certain you are you're right, there will still be a voice in your head screaming, "What are you doing? Are you out of your mind?" When that happens, go back and double-check, then triple-check, your facts. Is there anything you've missed? Anything you've overlooked? Are you engaging in wishful thinking? If you can, show your figures to someone you trust, someone with the expertise to tell you if your data paints the picture you think it does.

If everything checks out and you're determined to go big on your idea, then trust your data and make your move. Of course, writing that after the fact is a great deal easier than doing it at the time. When we began making offers on single-family homes, we were also taking on a great deal of personal financial risk, which led to high levels of stress and anxiety. By the time we bought our first round of properties, we had taken out about $15 million in loans and personally guaranteed them all.

We had both done well in our previous ventures and investments, but now we were risking a good portion of our net worth and guaranteeing away the rest, all while real estate prices were still in free-fall and the economy was on life support. During those early months, we were scared to death. A good night's sleep did not come easily, and it wasn't unusual for one or both of us to wake at night with a panic attack. Yes, we were confident in our model, but we also knew that we could be wrong.

Believing our data kept us focused and on track. We had hard numbers and had checked and rechecked them. We knew they were solid. We knew the opportunity was enormous. And as far as we could tell, no one else had seen it. There were no large-scale real estate investors probing the SFR market like we were. We ran into a few buy-and-flip investors on our fact-finding trips around the East Bay, but we never talked to anyone who was thinking in the direction we were or on the scale that we were. In fact, we met several flippers who couldn't believe we were buying and holding. For our part, we wondered why they would sell good real estate and face worse tax implications.

What we found didn't discourage us. If anything, it excited us. If you have plenty of solid data in front of you telling you something is a great opportunity and you're certain that you're interpreting it correctly, you don't need confirmation from ten other entrepreneurs that you're onto something. Anyway, somebody has to be first. We were hoping it was us.

## Beautiful Math

We made offers on a lot of houses. For every house we were able to buy, we made offers on dozens of properties. The first house we bought was in the city of Pittsburg, about forty miles northeast of San Francisco. It had been worth $410,000 in 2006, but now, in 2008, the bank was asking $85,000.

Think about that for a second. It's sobering. In just two years, this home had lost 80 percent of its value. Now imagine that you're the owners of this house. Perhaps you worked for years to be able to buy a nice home for your family, taking on a lot of debt but confident that you were getting into a stable market that would continue going up in value. All of a sudden you're $300,000 underwater and you've lost everything you worked for. Imagine the fear, the anger, and the resentment you would feel. Imagine the shame at getting that foreclosure notice in the mail. We never forgot that behind the shocking numbers in our database was a very human toll. That guided almost every business decision we made when we built Waypoint.

But at the moment, we had to buy some houses. We offered the bank $65,000 for that Pittsburg house. We were trying to get a sense of the market—looking for its *clearing price*, the price that reflects a rough balance between demand and supply. We didn't want to overpay, especially since we had the market to ourselves. But inexplicably, the bank turned down our offer. Then, as part of an automatic formula, a few weeks later, they lowered the asking price to $79,000.

In turn, we lowered our offer to $60,000. We were turned down again, and then the bank dropped the price to $72,500. *What the heck?* This made no sense. The bank owned this depreciating asset, and instead of selling it, they continued to devalue it and absorb the loss. Then the light bulb went off over our heads. *This* was why no one else was doing what we were doing. No one knew how to react to the killing field the Bay Area real estate market had become—not the banks, not real estate agents, not investors, nobody. There were no mathematical models that could predict ROI in that environment, and investors hate unpredictability. Meanwhile, the banks were taking on water from the enormous number of mortgage defaults. They were not lending to *anybody*.

Except us, that is. We were able to get debt. Without it, our story would have ended in 2009. First Republic Bank took a risk on us, even though they were refusing to lend money to house flippers and others. Why us? We weren't sure, but we had banked with them for years, and they knew us. More important, we showed up with a business plan filled with clear numbers that their risk managers could understand. We gave their underwriters a high degree of visibility into how these investments were likely to perform. We made them comfortable with our ability to execute. They, too, believed the data. First Republic deserves a lot of credit. They backed us when no one else would.

Those early First Republic mortgages came with interest rates of about 4 percent on seven-year fixed loans with a 50 percent loan-to-cost ratio. Loan-to-*cost*, not loan-to-*value*. For example, if we bought a $100,000 house, the bank would lend us $50,000. We would put $20,000 of our own capital into renovations, immediately making that house worth $120,000. But on the open market, it would sell for $150,000. So after renovations were complete, our loans with First Republic were effectively 33 percent loan-to-value for FRB.

We finally ended up paying $65,000 for that house, the same amount we initially offered. We had bought our first house! We kept making offers all over the area, looking at an endless parade of houses. But we were tormented by one question: "What are we missing?"

## Too Good to Be True?

The whole thing seemed too good to be true. We were looking at conservative underwriting numbers, and they were incredibly compelling. We were getting houses for 20 to 30 percent of what they had sold for in 2005 and expected to get 10 percent cash-on-cash returns. This looked like a once-in-a-lifetime chance to build something big. But was it possible that no one else was seeing what we were seeing? Could it be this easy? It didn't make sense.

"To play devil's advocate, I started proposing some alternate numbers," Colin says. "We were walking out of this house on Marks Boulevard in Pittsburg on Christmas Eve of 2008, and I said, 'I feel good about rent for this place at $1,500, but what if it was $1,400? Instead of being a 13 percent cap rate, that would give us a cap rate of 11 or 12 percent. Does that still work?'" (The "cap rate" is the unlevered yield on a property—the return when you ignore the debt.) The answer was a resounding yes!

Then we asked ourselves, "What if renovations cost us more than we think?" Instead of $20,000 for renovations, we plugged $30,000 into our model. Even with that higher cost, there was still plenty of profit. We looked at each other and realized that we could break every one of the assumptions in our underwriting model, get our costs wrong by 15 or 20 percent, and still make a terrific profit on each house.

Colin said, "I think I finally figured out what we're missing. The opportunity of a lifetime. We should just be buying more. If we get turned down at $70,000, we should be willing to pay $90,000. We should just be buying houses as fast as we can. The math was just that good." So that's what we did. We were ready to go long.

## Going All In

For the next six months, we put our heads down and made hundreds of offers on bank-owned properties in neighborhoods that we thought would give us the best possible ROI. Amazingly, we still had the market almost completely to ourselves. Our only competition was flippers, but flippers tend to think small, buying one or two houses—or if they're feeling daring, five houses—at a time. Flippers renovate, sell, pocket a profit, and move on.

That's nice, but it's limited. If you're really skilled at flipping and have a strong team of contractors, you might flip eight houses in a year and clear $400,000 in personal income if nothing goes wrong. But why follow that model when it means paying ordinary income taxes and selling a good house that's generating strong cash flow? It didn't make sense to us.

We had a great business model and a *system*. More important, we had scale in mind. We didn't want to buy five houses. We wanted to buy five hundred. In the years since, many flippers have told us that they regretted not doing what we did. We understood. Our way was unnerving and demanding. You needed access to capital and the ability to manage an operation.

Once we knew we could trust our dataset, we were all-in. We were getting seven- to ten-year fixed-rate loans, and we were happy to hold the properties and get the cash flow. We believed that when the economy bounced back, Bay Area real estate values would rebound strongly as well. Prices might drop in the near term, but in the long term, we would be collecting rent plus 5 to 10 percent annual appreciation, minimum. Even if we were wrong in the short term, we could afford to wait until we were right.

We put in one million dollars of our own money ($500,000 each) and borrowed another $1.5 million, and in six months, we had closed on twenty-six more houses. Because we wanted to be sure the market was what we thought it was, we also flipped a few as a sanity check. Could we really buy a distressed home for $100,000, put $20,000 into it to make it nice, and then sell it for $150,000?

We could. Buyers jumped at the nicely remodeled houses. They remembered that just two years earlier the same houses had been going for more than $400,000. Now we were certain we were right.

Those few months were fun. In flipping a few houses, we created value for buyers and banks. We made abandoned houses desirable and financeable, and we improved recession-battered neighborhoods. What was even better was proving that our model worked. Now we knew the potential was extraordinary. We decided to build something we could grow—something that would prove that SFR could become an institutional asset class.

In the early days of the business that would start out as DC Real Estate, we made water bottles that said "Forty or Bust" on them. Our go-big goal was to buy forty houses in a month and own one thousand houses. Everyone told us we were crazy.

They were right. It turned out to be *a lot* more than forty.

CHAPTER THREE

# Refine the System and Grow

Before we start to sound like fearless visionaries, let's be clear. We're fearful visionaries who happened to be at the right place at the right time, with the experience and combined skill set to take advantage of what we saw. We were also hungry for a big challenge and a great deal of work, but the timing was also perfect for us personally. If one or both of us had been in the middle of running our own companies, it's very possible that we would have said, "I'm tired just thinking about the work this would take, so forget it." However, we were both at a stage in our lives and careers where it seemed exciting to roll up our sleeves and work hard to take advantage of an incredible economic opportunity.

When it finally hit us that we were staring at the opportunity of a lifetime and that as far as we knew no one else had seen it yet, we resolved to move quickly. The sense that an extraordinary opportunity is at your fingertips is intoxicating. You might still have years of work in front of you to turn your idea into something big, but when an idea appears to be that much of a no-brainer, you're off to a good start.

However, the key word in our calculations was *yet*. As many bright business minds have pointed out, times of change and uncertainty are precisely when entrepreneurs find new opportunity . . . if they look for it. As Todd Krizelman, CEO of advertising intelligence company MediaRadar, said in *Forbes*, "Major upheavals may be unnerving, but they almost always open up a space for new entrants. Be agile and move in quickly; being early to market can be a major advantage." While we knew the SFR opportunity was unprecedented, we also knew that we would not have it to ourselves for long. It was simply too good. It might be a matter of a few months before the giant private equity investors (who had pockets much, much deeper than ours) came sniffing around. The time to go big and go long was now.

To accomplish that, one of the things we needed was a great core team. People have asked us how we were able to hire so many great people, because finding and keeping skilled, committed employees is a challenge for any company. Initially, it wasn't hard because the economy was bad and people were looking for work. But as the economy gradually improved and the job market with it, our people mostly stayed. Why?

When we hired our team, we told them up front that we would be asking them to work harder than they had ever worked in their lives. But nobody does that for money alone. People will go the extra mile when they feel like the company they work for is *worthy* of them, recognizes their value, and gives them a proving ground where they can be their best.

The reputation of Silicon Valley entrepreneurs is that we will sacrifice people in order to build a "unicorn" (a start-up with a billion-dollar valuation), but it's only the foolish ones who do that. Smart entrepreneurs know that without people to do the work, they have nothing. The real estate crash occurred in part because mortgage brokers and lenders stopped seeing borrowers as human beings and started viewing them as vehicles for their commissions. But we knew the value of great people, and we knew going long would only be possible if we brought some of them on board.

In the early days, one of our most important hires was Ali Nazar, who began as our chief technology officer and then transitioned to chief experience officer and who today is COO of our current company, Mynd. We knew that if we were going to go big, we needed a powerful technology back end, and Ali had both a marketing and a technology background, including expertise with the Salesforce platform. When Ali joined Waypoint in 2009, he had an unusual combination of roles: he worked on the backbone algorithm we used for underwriting and buying and also ran our marketing efforts. Ali also had a great ability not only to create technology but to really understand people's needs and how technology could be used to serve those needs. That's a rare combination of talents.

We managed to poach Ali from a struggling company, which ended up being a good move for us both. "I actually didn't get any money because we had to make payroll," Ali says. "Doug and Colin had, I think, twenty homes in their portfolio at the time, but they didn't know how to lease them. I helped them build a little technology solution for that. Then I decided to join a solar energy outfit and told Doug, 'Hey, you're going to have to find someone else to do this stuff.' Then he made a big offer to me to be their CTO, and I took the gig. That solar company went out of business a year later, and Waypoint did really well, so it was a good move on my part."

Ali took the lead in taking Waypoint from a sort-of-technology-driven company to a real proptech business. "I had this license to come in and really build a cutting-edge platform," he says. "That's what was really interesting to me about Waypoint. Doug was the real estate expert, Colin was the capital guy, so we were all very complementary parts, and together we were able to spin up a technology solution that automated all parts of the business.

"It ended up being a five-part solution, but I thought of it as five different businesses in one business," Ali goes on. "It was an acquisition engine. It was a renovation engine, a leasing engine, a property management engine, and a repairs and maintenance engine. All those things were tied together to provide one unified view of the life cycle of a property, from underwriting all the way to performing against the underwriting. It gave us a brilliant analysis of pro forma to actual. It was exciting because the technology started to become a key part of the fundraising story. We got really good at selling what we were doing, and I was really involved in all the fundraising. I had a tech demo that I called 'real estate porn.'

"I would come into a presentation with all these maps and bells and whistles, and I felt like the Wizard of Oz because most of these real estate equity investors and debt investors knew nothing about technology. I showed them some cool maps and some other cool stuff, and they were sold. They didn't know enough to ask me any questions. I was in a pretty good position because my job in fundraising was to make investors feel good, and I checked that box." Ali also became part of that close-knit tribe of key leaders we built that persists today, even though we've all scattered to different companies and parts of the country.

## Building Our First Fund

But even with Ali's software skills, scaling the business would be a demanding undertaking. Apart from the huge capital risk, we would have to model and build our own technology platform from the ground up while building a company whose business was based on continuously acquiring new properties for the foreseeable future. Over time, the business would become more complicated to manage, not less, and capital availability would be a constant issue. But there was never much doubt that we would do it. The economic opportunity justified the risk and the massive amount of work.

By the time we reached twenty-six homes in our portfolio, we hit a financial wall: no more capital to keep buying houses. At the same time, there were tens of thousands of undervalued single-family residences in the East Bay, and apart from us, practically no one was bidding on them. We said, "We have to scale this and do it quickly, but how?" The answer was clear: we would start our second fund—our first external fund.

We set out to raise $7 million.

First, we invested $500,000 from our personal wealth in the fund, and then we began reaching out to high-net-worth individuals who we thought might have an interest in investing in a real estate portfolio. We knew it would be easier to convince them to invest if they knew that we also had skin in the game. Of course, we were buying in a deep trough, so the risk wasn't as great as it seemed. Because we were borrowing just 50 percent of the cost of the homes, and because increasing their value was a simple matter of putting $20,000 into renovations, if we got into trouble, we figured we could sell some of the houses in our portfolio at a profit.

However, would there be people to buy the houses? Sure, we had been able to "test flip" two of our properties to prove the concept, but the real estate market was awash in fear and uncertainty at the time. Banks were running scared, so in order to get a loan, many of the buyers who would be shopping for homes in the working-class East Bay communities where we were buying would need 97 percent FHA loans. Those were going to be hard to come by in the unsteady economic conditions of the time.

In other words, it would be reckless for us to assume that we could quickly sell some of our portfolio to bail ourselves out of a cash crisis. We needed to make our idea work as a business. Having a company brand behind us would only make our work easier, so we tossed around a few name ideas. Eventually, in 2011, we would settle on Waypoint Homes, Inc. We felt that we could be a waypoint in our residents' lives, helping steer them in the right direction.

It was time to go back to our bankers at First Republic to see if they could help us out. They were willing to give us one-to-one financing: if we had $7 million in equity, they would give us $7 million in debt. That put us back in the acquisition business. But we had to move quickly. When you're raising millions from investors, the question everyone asks is, "How long will it take to

put the funds to work?" We needed to purchase enough properties to produce sufficient cash flow to keep the company running
while showing our investors a regular return on their investment.

In other words, to turn that $7 million in investor capital into
real estate, we needed people who would scout houses, make
offers, find renters, and manage our portfolio. We started leasing
office space and hiring a team. Before long, Waypoint had become
a fast-moving, complex machine with a lot of moving parts.

## The Model Takes Shape

Over the next few months, we were able to raise an additional
$6.5 million from high-net-worth individuals—people who saw
the same opportunity we did in the depressed East Bay real estate
market. With the $500,000 we had put in ourselves, that gave us
a fund of $7 million.

The fund had a seven-year target life with three one-year exten-
sions, so we could keep it open for up to ten years. The overall
vision we sold our investors was pretty simple: We would buy
homes and get perhaps a 10 percent annual cash-on-cash return
during the time we held them, and when we closed out the fund,
we would sell the homes. Because we bought them at historically
low prices in one of the most desirable real estate markets in
the country, they would have appreciated substantially, everyone
would get their profits, and we would get our fee. We structured
the fund to pay us a 2.5 percent management fee, and we would
also get 25 percent of the profits as long as our investors got at
least an 8 percent return.

This meant someone who invested $100,000 in our fund might
make $10,000 a year from his share of rents. Then, if the portfo-

lio of homes produced a compounding 20 percent internal rate of return (IRR, the annualized return rate) through appreciation, that investor would have more than doubled his money within five years. It was a very attractive business model. Now we had to put in the work to make it real.

The key was our technology-driven underwriting methodology, which we used to change the game and turn a mom-and-pop sector of the economy into an institutional asset class. As you probably know, underwriting uses data to determine the level of risk involved in an investment and, therefore, what you're willing to pay or lend for that investment. Our underwriting model was based on meeting a constant, tight time frame. As we said before, Waypoint was like a shark: we had to keep moving and buying homes to survive. When we closed on a house, our model dictated that we had to have it fully renovated and leased within ninety days. Thirty days to get all our renovations done, thirty days to get the property leased, and thirty days to get renters moved in and paying rent. That had to happen like clockwork.

Early on, meeting that goal was relatively easy. We would close on a house and have workers in it within days. They would do demolition—start with bigger jobs like roofing, plumbing, and electrical—and then move to finish work, paint, and landscaping. Over time, that turned into the standard renovation playbook for our houses.

Before too long, you could drive through the East Bay neighborhoods where the foreclosure bomb had gone off and immediately spot the Waypoint Homes. For one thing, they might be the only houses in good shape on a street where most of the other homes were in disrepair. They also tended to look alike because we used the same color paint, flooring, counters, ground cover, and the same skilled workers.

When you're working at high speed with high volume, find what works and replicate it. When in doubt, spend a little more for quality because that's going to keep your renters happy and save you from headaches in the long run. Because we made our renovation as formulaic as possible, our contractors were able to walk into a house, say, "Okay, what are we changing?" and get to work. They knew what we wanted, and that made the work go faster.

## Eating Our Own Dog Food

However, the key to making Waypoint scale was our technology platform, Waypoint Compass, which brought everything from underwriting all the way to renter service together in a single user interface.

Remember, investors had steered clear of single-family rentals for years because of the complexity and cost of managing a portfolio of individual properties scattered over a wide geographic area. The widespread belief was that managing hundreds or thousands of SFRs was like managing hundreds or thousands of small, one-family apartment buildings one at a time. Unlike managing hundreds of renters in a single apartment building or condo complex, such a business model would be incredibly inefficient, and inefficiencies were expensive.

To be fair, that skeptical belief might have been valid before the advent of wireless devices and cloud connectivity. But now, in Silicon Valley in 2009 and 2010, technology was changing the math. Our solution to the inefficiency of SFR was to tie everything together using technology and data. We brought mobile communications, the cloud, big data, and analytics to single-family rental real estate, a sector that's traditionally been a hands-on, mom-and-pop industry dominated by local landlords and local property management agencies. We used technology to create efficiencies by automating underwriting with a software algorithm, gathering neighborhood and property data systematically using mobile devices, and so on.

Our theory was that people had not failed to turn single-family units into a cohesive business because the sector was inherently unmanageable but because there were no tools to do it. We had the tools and a theory. This was the time to put it to the test—or, as we liked to say, to "eat our own dog food."

Eating your own dog food means test-piloting your idea on yourself to see if it works in the real world. Even the greatest idea is speculation until you find out if people will actually buy what you're selling—or, in our case, until we found out if our technology and model would consistently enable us to identify ideal single-family homes, buy them, and rent them profitably. No matter how smart you are, no matter how experienced your team is, no matter how brilliant your idea is, there's no substitute for getting into the field and stress testing your business.

We thought our data was sound and our model made sense, but until we'd actually put it to work with real money on the line, we couldn't be 100 percent certain that we were right. It is important to act decisively, but if you're not careful, you might let your enthusiasm blind you to the shortcomings in your business plan or overlook complications and variables until they hit you between the eyes.

In the worst-case scenarios, ego and greed lead some entrepreneurs to ignore obvious flaws and delude themselves (and others) into believing in a business that isn't what they claim it is.

Take Adam Neumann, the former CEO of WeWork. Instead of eating his own dog food, he drank his own Kool-Aid, convincing himself, the press, and investors (to the tune of a head-shaking $47 billion peak valuation) that he was reinventing society when he was just in the office space arbitrage business.

Don't assume you're right or that you're doing something that's never been done. Get into the field and test-drive your ideas when there's relatively little at stake so you can work out the bugs before you put everything on the line.

## Reinventing Underwriting

For us, the real test started with our technology-driven underwriting process. We were electronically connected to the MLS, so we knew the current and historical prices for the East Bay neighborhoods we were interested in. We had also gathered a great deal of data about our target neighborhoods, including crime rates, school quality, and median income. Some of it came from third-party sources, but we were also building our own proprietary dataset. We had Waypoint employees driving around these neighborhoods with laptops (and later iPads) and scoring them based on four characteristics:

- **Sights**. How does the neighborhood look? Are the homes well tended? Are there trees? Is the area clean, or are the front yards unkempt and the streetlights broken, with garbage everywhere?
- **Sounds**. Is the neighborhood quiet? Or is it located right near a busy freeway or maybe a sports stadium or something else noisy?

- **Safety**. Is it well lit at night? Are there people on the streets and the front porches? Do the police patrol regularly? Or is there graffiti, bars on the windows, and nobody on the streets after dark?
- **Surrounding use.** What's nearby? Is the neighborhood mostly residential, with perhaps a park and an elementary school nearby? Or is it near things that buyers don't like, such as a shopping mall or factory? Once, we accidentally bought a house that was sandwiched between a gas station and a porn shop. That was a fail.

We compiled those lifestyle factors into a proprietary *livability score*. The livability score was useful because it was house-independent. After all, we could renovate a house, but we couldn't change the neighborhood. We fed our livability data, along with our school, income, and crime data and our MLS information, into a custom-built algorithm, and that software automatically underwrote the house we were interested in. The smart system told us what we should pay for it based on the neighborhood, how much rent we could expect to get, and how much it was likely to appreciate per year. Making offers became much faster and easier with such precise data in hand. It wasn't guesswork anymore.

Objectively determining the desirability of a neighborhood helped us know where to invest. Our general philosophy was that we were willing to take lower returns in order to buy houses in higher-quality neighborhoods. Everything is a balance between current yield and appreciation. If you buy rentals in a bad neighborhood, you can expect greater profits on rents because your purchase price—and your carrying cost—should be lower. But your upside potential is also lower because homes in more run-down parts of town have low ceilings for appreciation.

If you invest a million dollars in real estate, you will get more current yield in a bad neighborhood than in a good neighborhood, but you will enjoy greater long-term appreciation in a good neighborhood, despite the houses being more expensive. That's why it's important to be clear about what your long-term goals are—and why the Bay Area market was so perfect for what we did.

In good times, Bay Area home prices are among the highest in the country, so in general, if you buy a rental property in and around San Francisco, your current yields will be lower than if you bought a rental somewhere else. However, by buying homes in relatively low-end neighborhoods of a region that still boasted a strong economy and job market (relative to the rest of the country at that time), we ensured that as the Bay Area economy improved in the coming years, our portfolio of homes would appreciate dramatically in comparison to other parts of the region. The rising tide would lift Waypoint's boat. Our automated system was designed to flag properties with the best mix of current yield and long-term appreciation.

## Squatters and Meth Labs

Of course, technology could only give us data. It wasn't a substitute for professional judgment. We had to put boots on the ground and eyes on the homes we wanted to buy. That meant we had to think about personal safety for the Waypoint employees who would be going into the field to check out potential purchases.

Desperation and economic stress breed crime, and there were some East Bay neighborhoods you just didn't go into because they were too dangerous. We didn't want to put our team at risk. That was another reason we were willing to take lower current yield to invest in better-quality neighborhoods: in the long run, those neighborhoods would cause us fewer problems with things like vandalism, theft, and 911 calls. So we definitely had some no-go neighborhoods labeled on our map.

But even in picking our spots and being careful, we saw humanity at its worst during those months crisscrossing the East Bay, when we were still doing a lot of the property reconnaissance ourselves. We found ourselves in some extremely sketchy neighborhoods, and because we always entered a house when we could to inspect it before we made an offer on it, those experiences were often quite unnerving. When homes were empty, they were usually boarded up, and there was no electricity. We skulked around with flashlights like characters from *The Walking Dead*, looking to see if the previous owners had vandalized the place beyond repair. It was creepy and depressing at times.

On plenty of occasions, we heard people dashing out of the back of a house just as we came in the front. One time, we even heard someone roaming around in the attic. Squatters were a huge problem during the financial crisis because in addition to the crush of loan defaults and foreclosures (according to RealtyTrac, US foreclosures went up 225 percent between 2006 and 2008), lots of other homeowners simply walked away from homes that were underwater or from mortgage payments that had gone up 200 or 300 percent overnight. There was a real human calamity happening in our area: thousands of families with nowhere else to go simply took possession of vacant houses because there was nobody to chase them away.

During the housing crisis, squatting became a huge problem all over the country as people lost their jobs and the value of their houses plummeted. One *Reuters* article from 2008 illustrates how extreme some of the behavior became:

> In some regions, squatting is taking on new twists to include real-estate scams in which thieves "rent out" abandoned homes they don't own. Others involve "professional squatters" who move from one abandoned home to another posing as tenants who seek cash from banks as a condition to leave the premises—a process known by real-estate brokers as "cash for key."

In our ventures into the suburbs, we also ran across a more common problem with vacant, boarded-up homes: the chronically homeless and drug users. On numerous occasions, we found drug paraphernalia in houses we were inspecting, and once we bought a house that had been used as a meth lab. It became a regular practice for us to scout a boarded-up house carrying baseball bats and to deliberately make lots of noise entering. Our biggest fear was we would surprise some guy who was high on drugs, who would then panic and become violent. We didn't want anyone to get hurt.

Perhaps the low point of these experiences came in 2009, when we witnessed a murder—sort of. We had just closed on a house in Pittsburg and were doing a walk-through to determine needed renovations. We were both upstairs by a window when we heard the unmistakable pop-pop-pop of gunfire. Startled, we looked out the window, where there was a park in front of the house. On the other side of that park, in the street, we could see a man lying in the street. We looked at each other and decided it was a good idea that we leave as quickly as we could. In the paper the next day, we read that the victim had been a good Samaritan who had been chasing down a robber until the robber turned around and shot him. It was a reminder that these times were chaotic and frightening.

Most of the neighborhoods we explored weren't that bad. Mostly what we saw in the vacant homes we toured was evidence of neglect, desperation, and anger, from vandalism to meals left half-eaten as the former owners packed up and left. The saddest things were always the toys: perfectly good children's toys that had been left behind. We always wondered what would cause someone to leave so abruptly that they left their kids' toys too. We always made sure to gather that stuff up and put it in the garage in case the owners came back looking for it. Once we even found a fish tank with fish still swimming around in it. Doug brought them home and had his daughter care for them.

Sometimes we were disgusted by what we saw. Sometimes we were shocked. Mostly, we were saddened.

## Slumber Party Security

Even after we owned the houses, our problems with squatters didn't stop. We needed bodies on-site who could be checking our houses and alerting us to problems. Then one day Doug had a brainstorm. He'd played football at Cal and stayed close to the people running the program, and they told him about a former wide receiver named Alex who had just graduated. Doug tracked him down and said, "You want an internship?"

Alex did. He was a great kid and interested in real estate. We didn't offer to pay him at first, but we told him that if he worked out, in three or four months, we would start paying him. Alex became our "possession receiver" of sorts. As soon as we closed on a property, he would go out and take physical possession of it. If there were squatters, it was his job to make sure they left and ensure that the house was physically secured against unlawful entry.

Of course, that was easier said than done. This poor kid dealt with some crazy situations. Once, when he was walking into a house, he heard the back door slam open. Alex sprinted toward the backyard and saw a naked man running through the unmowed grass toward the fence. Alex instinctively started chasing the guy and was about to grab him as he tried to scale the back fence of the property. He only stopped short when he realized, as he told us, "I'm about to grab this naked man by his bare butt! What am I doing?" Even though it was no laughing matter, we had to laugh. As far as we know, the man never came back, and that's all we were concerned with.

Some squatters were more intrepid. They were relentless and saw our properties as *their* homes; no matter how often we chased them away, they would sneak back in the middle of the night. For example, the daughter of the former owner of one of our homes kept breaking in over and over again, insisting that she had squatter's rights and saying, "This house is ours." She would even break in while renovation was underway, and each time we would ask her to leave. Sometimes we'd call the police, but they generally had other matters to deal with, so we were on our own. We worried that eventually someone, maybe one of our contractors, would get hurt.

We finally realized that in order to overcome the squatter problem, we had to take more radical measures. So Alex recruited a bunch of his fellow former Cal football players, and we had them sleep at our houses every night until renovations were done.

Imagine, if you will, the world's largest slumber party for the world's biggest kids. If you had looked through the windows on those nights, you would have seen all these huge dudes scattered all over the upstairs on foam mattresses and sleeping bags, watching movies and scarfing down pizza. It cost us about one hundred dollars per night per player (football players can eat a lot of pizza), but that was a bargain price for having our own private security force.*

At a time when America was drowning in bad debts and broken promises and when nobody knew what the rules were for real estate now that everything had come crashing down, the downtrodden neighborhoods of the East Bay were like our own Wild West. That was the environment in which we laid the foundation for our company.

## Forrest Gump Real Estate

In the second half of 2009 as we were buying houses left and right, we also started to hire more people. We had already hired folks like Kevin Fulton, our first employee and construction manager, while we were buying our initial twenty-six homes. As we were raising fund two, we started growing in earnest. We were navigating two worlds at the same time. We would put on suits, go to the bank and speak with private investors to raise capital, and then pull off our ties and jackets, throw on jeans, grab our bats and flashlights, and head back out into the ghostly world of abandoned properties.

By the end of that early expansion phase, we had bought one

---

* Interestingly, one of our football player security guards was Tosh Lupoi, who played at Cal, went on to be a coach at Cal, became defensive coordinator for the University of Alabama (building a reputation as one of the best college football recruiters in America), and today is the defensive line coach for the Jacksonville Jaguars.

hundred and four more homes. As we gathered more and more data using technology, we followed the same methodology we'd followed in buying our first twenty-six homes: focusing on working-class neighborhoods and staying near the BART line.

However, relying on our data also led us to buy a lot of homes in Vallejo, a navy city of 125,000 people on San Pablo Bay. Prices were even lower there than they had been in Pittsburg and Antioch, which probably had something to do with the fact that the city had filed for bankruptcy in May 2008. We also bought along the Interstate 880 corridor, which runs through working-class cities like Hayward, Fremont, and San Leandro.

We were beginning to build a reputation, especially among real estate brokers. They were panicked and desperate after the crash because nothing was selling and the only people buying were investors like us. This was understandable. If you were a real estate agent in Vallejo in 2005, you might sell five houses a month at $400,000 each and collect a $12,000 commission on each one. Even if you had to split that commission fifty-fifty with your broker, you were still making $30,000 a month—$360,000 a year. You're driving a Benz and living the high life. Fast-forward to 2008, and your average sale has dropped to $75,000, and that's assuming you can even *find* buyers for your listings. When we started networking with brokers and agents to ask about buying all their listings, they were more than eager to talk to us.

One broker called us and made a pretty strange sales pitch. "I have this house," she said. "It's a total disaster. It's in a terrible neighborhood. You want to look at it?" How could we turn down a pitch like that? Well…she hadn't been kidding. The house was in the worst part of Vallejo, literally next to the railroad tracks in an area that was also a homeless camp. The house itself had been wrecked by squatters and the previous owners, and it smelled so bad that it was hard to even go near it. The good news was that the house was priced at $26,000. Imagine paying that much for a four-bedroom, two-bathroom, two-thousand-square-foot house in the Bay Area. Talk about a bargain!

We bought it, and when we got a renovation crew in there, the condition of the place was even worse than we expected it to be. Plus, while we tried to figure out how much it would cost us to renovate the place and what we might be able to rent it for, we had another challenge: keep the homeless from taking up residence while our contractors were working.

We did the numbers and got a crew of guys working on the house, but after just two days, our general contractor came to our rescue. He told us he wanted to buy the house as-is. He didn't know how much we paid for it, but he said, "This house is a big project, but I have a whole bunch of guys, and I could take care of this." We sold it to him for $75,000, tripling our money in less than a month.

That's what the Bay Area market was like then. It was Forrest Gump real estate: every deal was like a box of chocolates, and you didn't know what you were going to get.

One house at a time, we built our portfolio. Our automated underwriting system crunched the numbers, and we had an acquisition team in the field making offers. It was a ton of work, but we got some incredible deals. We had to be sharpshooters, following our model to the letter and buying the best houses in the best locations.

We also bought one home at a time because we needed our portfolio of homes to be relatively close together on the map. Once they were renovated and occupied, we had to manage them, and if we had homes located from San Jose in the south all the way up to San Rafael, we would end up with unsustainable costs for simple management and maintenance calls.

We could have bought homes in bulk if we had been willing to buy at Fannie Mae auctions of foreclosed homes. However, we avoided those auctions because the portfolios frequently consisted of a lot of bad houses with a few good ones mixed in. We tested the Fannie Mae auction waters once and bought twenty-five homes at a shot, but that auction gave us our biggest disaster of those early days. Our acquisitions guy was bidding on properties for us at a Fannie Mae auction, and later in the day, he called us and said, "I have good news and bad news. The good news: we got the deal."

Well, that was great! What was the bad news? "Uh, somehow, we accidentally sent the wrong offer price in."

Accidentally? An accident is when you break a wineglass or forget your car keys. Through this guy, we had overpaid for one of the houses in the Fannie Mae portfolio by $100,000! Needless to say, that was his last day at Waypoint, but now we had to figure out what to do with the property. We couldn't go to Fannie Mae and ask them to let us out of the deal because we were trying to build a good relationship with them.

Our only choice was to bite the bullet. We put $100,000 of our own money back into the fund to make it right for our investors and then spent a year unloading all the other poor-quality homes in that Fannie Mae portfolio. Chastened by the experience, we didn't dare deviate from our business model again for a while.

But eventually, hungry for growth, we did, and that got us into more trouble than we could have possibly imagined.

CHAPTER FOUR

# We Get Investigated by the FBI

From the beginning of Waypoint, we tried to be guided by principle as much as the desire for growth. After all, in the end, you are either someone who can be trusted to do the right thing or you're not. If you combine a good idea and a lot of hard work with being honest and treating people with respect, you stand a good chance of being successful. Whatever your core principles are, if they've worked for you and you've been successful because of them, why would you ever violate them?

With Waypoint, one of our core business principles was to build our solutions with our own hands so we could keep control of them. For example, when we built our automated underwriting system, we didn't use off-the-shelf software, which is what our later competitors did. We built our algorithm by hand and set up the entire system to give us precisely the analytics that we needed to make the best possible investment decisions. That paid off in the growth we saw from 2008 to 2010.

However, by late 2009, what we expected to happen happened: single-family home prices started to go up in the East Bay. Not by much—they were still at near-historic lows. But because the first houses we bought were so cheap, prices had nowhere to go but up. The other reason prices were rising was competition. Other investors and larger PE funds had finally gotten wind of the opportunity and were beginning to bid on homes in our target areas, which also put upward pressure on home prices. Between bidding wars and having to work harder to close on homes, our rate of acquiring new properties slowed, and our business model depended on a near-constant influx of new houses.

As 2010 began, we were starting to look at raising our fourth fund from high-net-worth investors. However, it's worth remembering that putting that new capital to work meant continuously growing our real estate portfolio. It was time for us to explore other ways to buy houses apart from the MLS. That led us to venture into an area we had long avoided—foreclosure auctions. Auctions would allow us to buy on another new channel, which would keep the flow of new properties going. But what we really bought were more headaches than we ever thought possible.

## Foreclosure Auctions: A Sketchy World

You're probably familiar with these auctions. Banks (not to mention federally sponsored loan guarantors like Fannie Mae) that have taken possession of foreclosed homes eventually decide to sell these nonperforming assets at foreclosure auctions. If you have access to capital and can handle managing multiple properties, you might buy twenty homes or more with a single bid. But as you can imagine, when the potential to land incredible deals is high, the interest and competition become intense.

Buyers literally gather on the steps of county courthouses, and an auctioneer works his way through a list of foreclosed properties and groups of properties. What you probably don't know, and what we did not know at the time, is that courthouse auctions are often a rigged game. When we spoke to knowledgeable colleagues about auctions, they told us to avoid them. They told us there were five or six investors and companies that controlled the auction activity in the Bay Area—a group known as the "Courthouse Mafia."

We started buying at auctions before we really knew what we were getting into, but when we started meeting auction veterans, the stories they told were appalling. If you were a new buyer at a courthouse auction, crooked auctioneers getting kickbacks from buyers might whisper as the bids came in so only the people at the front of the group could hear. Before you could object, they'd yell, "Sold!" Bid rigging, where multiple parties collude to decide who will submit the winning bid while the other bidders deliberately submit low bids or don't bid at all—the auction equivalent of price fixing—was common, despite being illegal.

Later we also found out that illegal secondary auctions were also common. A few parties would choose a designated buyer to buy a house for the opening price. The auctioneer would start the bidding, the chosen buyer would bid, and everyone else would stay silent. The house would sell for a rock-bottom price, and after the auction, the conspirators would gather privately and hold their own auction of that property.

We heard horror stories about new buyers who bought more properties than the Courthouse Mafia was comfortable with, and when they went to inspect their new purchases, they found the houses had been severely vandalized. We heard about auctioneers who'd been beaten because they'd stepped on someone's toes. This was serious business.

Auction veterans advised us that if we were determined to buy in bulk at auctions, we should not wade into that world on our own. Instead, it was suggested that we hire a company or an individual with experience in buying homes at auction for investors. Such people, we were told, knew all the tricks, knew how to spot crooks, and knew how to get results while working within the laws. We thought about it and agreed that it might be a good idea. But we were walking into a trap. For the first time since starting Waypoint, we were about to violate our "build the solution yourself" principle.

Undaunted, we started interviewing potential buying partners. The person we hired would be our proxy on the courthouse steps, using his or her years of auction experience to make bids and buy homes on our behalf. The idea was that this would help protect our investors' money while reducing our risk of potentially being caught up in something illegal or unethical. While we were interviewing such individuals, an unfortunate event drove home how inexperienced we were and how badly we needed expert assistance. We bought a house at an auction on our own, but somehow we got the property address mixed up.

After the deal closed, we sent a construction crew over to the property to begin renovations. A few days later our construction manager came to the office and said, "We have a little problem. You want the good news or the bad news?"

By now, we had grown to hate this question. We asked for the bad news.

"We just did a $25,000 renovation on a house that we don't own."

Whoops. What was the good news?

"We did it really fast."

"That's good news?"

We had gotten the incorrect address from the auction company. Veterans know that you should never trust the address given on the courthouse steps. You should always match the address with the auction ID number. But we didn't know that then, so we didn't do it. As it turned out, the house we *thought* we'd bought was also boarded up and had been foreclosed on, because that was common in those days. In the end, the bank that owned the house got $25,000 in free renovations. Even though we tracked that house to bid on it at auction, for some reason, it never went under the auctioneer's hammer. Once again, we had to put our own cash in the fund to make it right because that was too big a mistake for our investors to eat. Obviously, if we were going to make auctions profitable, we needed professional assistance.

## Deals with the Devil

Getting involved in auctions also showed us that buying properties that fit the precise parameters of our model was going to be more complex and time consuming than we had realized. When we got the list of properties to be auctioned on a given day, our people had to determine a baseline value for each one, pull and analyze title reports, drive to the properties and inspect them, and get checks to our bidders. We also found out that a bank could pull a property from the auction at any time with no notice, which meant that our bidder might show up at the courthouse only to find out that the houses we wanted weren't going under the hammer at all. This happened to us almost daily. The whole affair consumed time that our staff could have been using to make other offers and to manage our growing portfolio of SFRs.

We needed someone knowledgeable who could do all that legwork for us. We met a guy who had the right background, but we couldn't get him to give us a price. He would say things like, "What I pay for a house should have nothing to do with what you pay for it. You tell me what it's worth," or, "You tell me the most you'll pay in advance, and then I'll go buy it. If I make twenty grand on it, good for me."

We had no interest in doing that. We told him we were buying on behalf of a pool of investors and planned to do a lot of volume, so we needed predictable numbers. "Let's just agree to a dollar amount that we'll pay you per house," we said. He was having no part of it. However, this guy really knew his stuff, so we said, "Let's try one house." He bought one for us, but then he wouldn't tell us how much he paid for it. We did our research and figured out that he was going to make between $10,000 and $15,000 on this one house. That was unacceptable. We were not about to let a contractor dictate the terms of our business dealings. We decided not to use him.

Finally, we settled on a man we will call Blake Weiss. He was more polished than our previous candidate and was willing to agree on a flat fee. Assuming the house was as advertised, we would pay him $5,000 for every house he bought for us on the courthouse steps—at or below our maximum price—once the deal closed.

Blake's job was to drive around to all the houses on the next week's auction list and inspect them. You never knew which ones the banks might pull at the last minute, so you had to look at them all. But when a house is a bank-owned foreclosure, you can't go inside. You can only make your best guess about its condition from the exterior, the yard, and the neighborhood. Remember the reality show *Storage Wars*? Those antique dealers and resellers would line up outside of seized storage units and bid on the contents sight unseen, based on the clues they could see from a brief, hands-off look at the contents. But they couldn't go inside the units. As a result, sometimes they bought treasures, and sometimes they bought trash. This was like that.

The really shady operators had their ways of getting a look inside the houses, but we didn't allow that; it was trespassing. But even with the restrictions, Blake started buying homes for us and was good at it. But he was always a bit sketchy too. He bought more than one hundred houses for us, but every so often it was like a voice in his head said, *I'm giving Doug and Colin too good of a deal,* and he would try to renegotiate his terms. Once, he disappeared for a week, and it turned out that he had a drug problem. But we stuck with him because he was doing a good job, buying us good houses at good prices.

This was the one time in our journey from Waypoint to Mynd that our hunger for growth overruled one of our other core principles: *Work with good people.* When you're poised to go long and make a big bet on an opportunity, it can be tempting to throw everything over the side of the boat so you can grow, grow, and grow some more. Don't give in to that temptation. Stick to the values that got you where you are. Never forget that good people are your greatest asset, bad people can become your greatest liability, and values do matter.

During the years we ran Waypoint, we worked hard to hire good people, compensate them well, and build a strong, tight-knit team. Especially among our senior executives, but throughout the company, there was a real "we're family" feeling that persists to this day. We're really proud of the bond we still share with people who were at Waypoint from the beginning. We all felt like we were working hard to build something exceptional. We focused on hiring people of strong character whom we could trust to execute our model.

Blake was good at buying houses, but he wasn't that trustworthy, and we had doubts about his character. But we ignored the signs that we'd made a deal with the devil.

Then in mid-2010, when we owned about three hundred houses, a friend of ours called us and said, "I just got served a subpoena for the courthouse steps. Blake Weiss has been arrested, and they're subpoenaing everyone involved, all the buyers. It's a massive federal investigation. Your former buyer is the kingpin, and all your buying entities are on the subpoena list. Just wanted to give you guys a heads up. I think you're going to be getting a visit from the FBI."

## The Big Fish

In fact, we had fired Blake about six months before, which was a relief. But we were also nervous because he had bought about one hundred houses for us. Mostly, we kicked ourselves for going against our do-it-yourself ethos and farming out an important part of our business model. As a result, we had invited who-knew-what kind of chaos and liability into our lives. Since 2008, we had been right again and again about the SFR market, and

Waypoint had been flying high. But entrepreneurship will usually find a way to humble you. Never forget that you *can* be wrong, you *will* be wrong, and you're just as capable of making a bad call as anyone else.

Blake had been arrested for bid rigging, which is a federal offense. In bid rigging, a bidder might bribe other bidders not to bid on a house, pay an auctioneer to ignore bids, or get other bidders to submit noncompetitive bids. Bid rigging is anticompetitive collusion that reduces the sale price of houses, which means it harms consumers and taxpayers. Blake was in big trouble—and as his biggest client, we were afraid that we were too, even though we hadn't known what he was doing. Colin walked into the office the next morning, and our receptionist said, "The FBI is here. I put him, the guy, in your office. He's waiting to meet with you."

Wow. Okay. *This just got real. Deep breath.*

Colin went into the office, sat down with the FBI agent, and said, "How can I help you?"

"I'd like to ask you some questions. Do you know Blake Weiss?" Right to the point, all business.

"Yes. He's a consultant who worked for us, to help us buy houses on the courthouse steps."

"You know, he's suspected of bid rigging. Do you know anything about this?"

"No."

That was just the beginning. The agent asked a bunch more questions and then handed Colin a subpoena on the spot. The subpoena entitled the FBI to copies of our records, emails, telephone records, and anything else pertinent to the case. They were asking for a massive quantity of documents and data, and we knew it would take months to compile it all. We started to worry that this was quite serious for us. Then we spoke to Doug's wife, Shanti, a top-flight criminal defense attorney and author of *Almost Innocent*, and became even more concerned.

You know that moment when you or a loved one gets a diagnosis of a serious health problem? All you want is for the doctor to tell you, calmly and matter-of-factly, that he's seen hundreds of cases like this before and everything is going to be all right. That's what we were hoping for when Doug told Shanti that our auction agent had been arrested and the FBI had subpoenaed us. Who better to turn to than a defense attorney for some calming perspective on a legal dilemma? But Shanti did not calm our nerves. Instead, she became deeply concerned.

"The FBI does not screw around," she said. "You guys both need attorneys. Get them fast. Don't talk to anyone. Don't even talk to each other about this. You guys have to do this right. This is a machine that you're caught in now."

Later, we found out that more than one hundred people had gotten subpoenas from the feds and that multiple parties, not just Blake, were suspected of rigging bids. This was a huge investigation, and the FBI wasn't just after the guys who were rigging bids on the courthouse steps. Those were the foot soldiers, the small fish. The FBI was after the big fish: the investors who had directed their proxy bidders to rig auctions, falsify bidding, and defraud the banks and the taxpayers. In other words, Uncle Sam was after guys like us.

## It's About Numbers, Not Justice

The calendar flipped to 2011, and we knew that we had to lawyer up. But we wanted our lawyers to work together. We had become good friends, and this was a test of the strength not only of our partnership but of our friendship. We were afraid that with the right threats, the FBI could get one of us to say something that could be twisted into evidence against the other. We intended to stick together.

We hired Barry Bonds's former attorney, Cris Arguedas of Arguedas, Cassman, Headley, and Goldman. Cris was (and still is) well known in the Bay Area as one of the best criminal defense attorneys in the business. She and a highly-recommended colleague became our dream team. At the same time, we had to start providing the FBI with the thousands of electronic records and physical documents that their subpoena had demanded. Our people continued to manage our existing portfolio of rentals, but our well-oiled property underwriting and acquisition machine ground to a halt. Instead, we worked all day, every day, collecting all the communications the feds were asking for. It would end up taking us about six months to compile it all, and meanwhile, we were spending hundreds of thousands of dollars on legal fees while accomplishing less than we wanted for our business. It was incredibly frustrating.

To top it off, Cris let us know that we were in real legal jeopardy. One day she sat us down in her office and told us that the prosecutors had our contract with Blake, our back-and-forth communications, and the fact that he was buying properties for us with our money. It would be easy for them to presume that not only did we know there were shady dealings on the courthouse steps but that we had directed Blake to engage in illegal activities on our behalf. Our blood ran cold as she informed us that, like it or not, we were the big fish in this case. We were the biggest buyers at the courthouse and prominent business owners.

The US attorney was likely to charge us, she said, and if we were convicted, we were looking at federal prison time, not to mention losing our company.

We listened, horrified, as Cris told us that the prosecution would probably offer us a plea bargain—five to ten years in prison if we fought the charges and lost but only twelve to eighteen months if we plead guilty. She told us that even if we thought we had a 75 percent chance of winning the case in court, if we were not certain we would win, we should strongly consider taking a plea bargain, because if we bet everything in court and lost, we could be behind bars until our kids were out of high school.

We sat there in shock, not wanting to believe what we were hearing. We were two guys trying to grow a business, who were trying to create a path back to homeownership for families gutted by the foreclosure crisis. How could it be possible that we might have to plead guilty and spend time in prison to avoid an even longer sentence? We hadn't done anything except show poor judgment in hiring Blake! Didn't being innocent count for something?

If that sounds naïve, that's because we *were* naïve. We're not now. Over the next two years, we came to understand that the criminal justice system has nothing to do with justice. That's just the window dressing. Once you're caught in the gears of the machine, the interest of the people who run that machine isn't finding the truth. It's getting convictions. It's boosting their numbers. It's advancing their careers. The very worst thing you can do if you're in potential trouble with the law is say, "They can't do anything to me because I'm innocent." That's a dangerously cavalier attitude that can cost you dearly.

An academic study published in 2013 in the journal *Criminal Justice Ethics* backs up this perception with facts. The researchers found that the American criminal justice system is full of incentives for false convictions and that police, forensic scientists, and prosecutors often have strong incentives to get convictions while having little incentive to expend the resources to convict the right person or exonerate the wrongly accused.

If you talk to defense or appellate attorneys or search press coverage of court proceedings, it's easy to find case after case where innocent people got stuck in the system, victims of circumstances and of cops and prosecutors eager to earn promotions. (Shanti even wrote a book on the topic called *Almost Innocent*.) Some of those people were forced to plead guilty to things they hadn't done to avoid long prison sentences, often because they didn't have the financial resources to fight the government, which has near-unlimited resources. We were fortunate enough to be able to afford top legal counsel, but our pockets weren't bottomless. If things dragged out long enough, would we be forced to take a plea deal to avoid financial ruin?

## Two-and-a-Half Years of Hell

As 2011 turned into 2012 and the investigation dragged on, we also faced another tough reality: we were going to have to try to raise another fund! The capital we had raised from GI Partners and from fund number four had all gone to buy homes—to feed the shark. Now, in mid-2012, with our Wells Fargo deal dead, we were about three months away from having no more cash to run Waypoint. We would have to start working on fund number five.

Immediately, our attorneys warned us, "You guys can't go raise money. You shouldn't be taking on debt. You could get charged any day now." Instead, we disclosed to our investors everything that was happening. We expected some of them to be angry and suspicious, so we were surprised and gratified to find out that most were willing to stand by us and remain invested in our funds. In fact, through the entire FBI affair, we never lost an investor from any of our funds.

However, we had to drastically slow our buying, which was a huge risk, because our lifeblood was a continuous stream of new homes. We also worried that our banks, which were loaning us half the capital for this next fund, would turn off the flow of debt. Who would lend to business owners who'd been subpoenaed? We even started laying off Waypoint employees in anticipation of lean times.

Our situation was grim. If we didn't get a cash infusion, we would have to close down normal operations in ninety days. We would go into babysitting mode, stopping all buying activity but keeping a skeleton crew of key employees to manage our existing portfolio. We would set up Waypoint as a self-running operation for seven years, which would allow our existing funds to complete their contracted terms while our real estate appreciated. Eventually, Waypoint would sell the homes and give our previous investors their profits. It was a modest outcome compared to what we wanted, but what else could we do?

Well, we should have talked to our bankers first. It would have eased our minds. When we told our contacts at Citibank and our other lenders that we had been subpoenaed by the FBI, they laughed. They said, "Guys, people get subpoenaed all the time. This isn't a big deal." They were still willing to lend us capital, which meant we could keep Waypoint going while the investigation wound its laborious way along. That was one of the only blessings of that period: We had tried to do things the right way, and our financial partners recognized that. It made things a little bit easier.

However, as 2012 crawled along, a dark cloud of possible prison and ruin hung over us, causing us both a great deal of personal stress. There were a lot of sleepless nights. After we turned all our emails and other documents over to our attorneys, they said, "This is kind of concerning." There were exchanges in which we'd talked about how Blake seemed shady, and we were told that a prosecutor could have taken those as signs of a conspiracy. Cris also pointed out that because Blake was a relatively small fish, there was every chance that he would throw us under the bus to save his own skin. He had every incentive to make up a story about us in order to get a reduced sentence, and we should be ready for that. She was preparing us for the worst, and after a while, we started to expect it. We felt like someone was standing over us with a sword raised over our necks.

The year passed, and nothing else happened, which was somehow worse than getting bad news. We could fight a legal battle, but the information vacuum just led to more worry and stress. Meanwhile, our lawyers would regularly say things like, "I think you guys are going to get charged. Be prepared for this. This is how it's going to go down…" We were told that when they finally decided to arrest us, the feds would show up at our offices in the morning. When they did, we were to say nothing and call Cris right away. Meanwhile, we started imagining how we would tell our kids that their fathers were going to prison. We couldn't help it. It was hell, waiting for something terrible to happen when we knew the only thing we were guilty of was felony bad judgment.

## Gary Beasley

While all this was happening, we were making plans to save our company. Apart from securing capital, we knew that if we were charged—or worse, went to prison—we needed a firm hand on the wheel at Waypoint. We had our families and employees to think about, and if the worst happened and we did go to prison, we would need a life after we got out. We spent 2012 building our dream team to make sure we were ready for a worst-case scenario.

First, we promoted our third partner, Gary Beasley, to CEO. Gary was originally a managing director of Waypoint, then CEO of Waypoint, then co-CEO of Starwood Waypoint (patience, we'll tell you about this in Chapter 6), and he's now the CEO of Roofstock, another real estate tech start-up. He's also a good friend. Ultimately, we all ended up buying a ski house in Lake Tahoe together, which we still own.

When Gary joined Waypoint at the end of 2011, he added value in many critical ways. When we began trying to raise funds through private equity, it was clear that neither of us knew enough about it. Gary came on board at the perfect time and helped us accelerate our capital raising through private equity and, ultimately, through the public markets. He brought a formidable amount of public company and capital markets experience and credibility to the table, and that made him invaluable to us as we grew.

"Doug first brought up the idea to me at a girls' soccer tournament," Gary says. "We were shooting the breeze, and he started talking about wanting to buy homes in Pittsburg as investment homes. The whole time he was talking, I thought he was talking about Pittsburgh, Pennsylvania, not Pittsburg, California. I was thinking, *Why the hell is Doug in Pittsburgh?* We talked about it for about two weeks before I finally realized what he was talking about."

When we got past that geographic misunderstanding, Gary was intrigued by the rental yield that could be generated on the homes we were buying. "Prices had dropped at that point about 60 to 70 percent, and rents hadn't dropped, so Doug's whole thesis made sense," Gary says. "If you could generate a current yield and wait for the California real estate market to come back, you can't lose money on these things. I agreed with it. So I said, 'Listen, if you put together an LLC, I'll get some buddies to invest.'"

With Gary's help, we built some of our early funds with fifteen or twenty high-net-worth investors. "It just made so much sense," Gary says. "Then they asked me to be a part of their advisory board, so I stayed close to it for a couple of years. Then in the fall of 2011, I got a call from Doug and he said, 'We're starting to get some unsolicited term sheets from private equity investors and institutional investors who want to give us money. We'd like to go big with this thing, and we'd love to get your thoughts.' Well, sure."

We sent over a couple of term sheets, and after Gary looked them over, he called us. "I said, 'Guys, these are legitimate firms and real terms,'" Gary says. "'I think you need to think about this hard. Do you want to own a 100 percent of something and keep it small, or do you want to go big? If you want to go big, you're eventually going to lose control, but you could build a big platform and leave a mark on the industry.' They said they had thought about it already and they wanted to go big. And then they told me, 'You speak private equity, so we want you to come do this with us and be our third partner.'"

Gary said yes. He also experienced firsthand the recurring Waypoint pattern of trying to build the wings of the plane while it's in the air, always being three inches from financial disaster because of our cash burn rate. There was a great deal of intensity and adrenaline in those days, and while it was certainly not intentional, it was a natural offshoot of trying to go long and move fast.

"Our intention was not to bring the business to the brink of extinction," he says, "we just had confidence and a drive for success. Doug, being an athlete, has this work ethic and this belief that if you can't go over the wall, you go through it. There was confidence that we would always find a solution. That drive was instrumental in growing as fast as we did, even as we were running out of money. I think putting yourself in a position to be successful, you have to be willing to face that cliff and say, 'Well, if we can't raise money, we're done.' Most people would not accelerate toward that cliff, and that's what's so unusual about Doug and Colin. They have this belief, 'We're going to do it and we're going to figure it out.'"

## Charles Young

The other key "get" for our 2012 dream team was Charles Young, who ultimately became our high-caliber chief operating officer. He stayed on with Starwood Waypoint after Colin left, and is now the COO of Invitation Homes. Charles would have been a tough get for a young company under normal circumstances. He was about forty-five years old, a Stanford graduate with a master's in economics, and a former professional football player like Doug with a solid-gold résumé building high-profile developments.

When we approached Charles, he had already flipped a lot of multitenant buildings and single-family homes, and he saw what Waypoint was doing as a long-term flipping play. But after we explained the business model to him, he said, "Do I raise a $50 million fund myself or join you guys as regional director of Chicago?" When we talked with him for this book, he said that he was intrigued by our plans to professionalize the mom-and-pop real estate space but that what really intrigued him was our plans to, as he put it, "use technology to shrink time and distance." He also liked the idea of building a large portfolio of real estate with a national footprint. So he met with Gary Beasley to talk through the opportunity.

"Gary and I had a good conversation around how he saw the industry," Charles said. "He's very thoughtful and can be very convincing, and he planted the idea in my head that the universe of single-family rentals is large, somewhere between twelve and sixteen million homes. It was an interesting meeting, and when I went home, I couldn't sleep. I woke up and said, 'Sixteen million? We only need a little bit of this.' When do you have an opportunity to get in early and shape an industry? I said, 'Why not bet on myself and make this industry better?' That's how I said let's go." Charles then met Doug at a bar in Chicago, where Doug pitched him hard and convinced him to join Waypoint in June 2012. We were building quite a leadership team.

In the end, Charles loved our vision and values, and we were lucky to get him. He could be a slick politician and was great with people, but he also had a relentless work ethic, loved accountability, and was terrific at pushing an operation forward in an elegant, effective way. As we scaled the company up to thirteen markets and more than five hundred employees, he was one of our key guys. He ran Chicago and then the West Coast for us (our expansion comes later in this tale).

Charles was there for the growth and the intensity and the risk of what we were doing with Waypoint. In his words, we were inventing and building the plane while we were flying it. When we talked for this book, he told us that the value was in the discovery—learning the right neighborhoods, where we wanted to buy and why. He points out that we were trying to get to scale while working with less money than Blackstone and Invitation Homes but that our technology helped to level the playing field.

To this day, Charles still recognizes the quality of the model we were building back then. "It still resonates," he says. "There's still nothing better than buying the right house in the right neighborhood. I liked that we were doing that."

## The Unthinkable

By bringing in Charles and promoting Gary, we were setting up a first-rate leadership team that could take the reins of Waypoint and continue growing it. And as 2012 became 2013 and we still had never heard a word from the Department of Justice, we did our best to ignore the doom and gloom, keep raising capital, and grow the company.

We had closed nearly $300 million in debt with Citibank the previous October, but we knew that with what seemed like an endless need to grow our portfolio of homes, we would burn through that cash quickly. So we resumed talking with institutional investors.

In the process, we disclosed everything. We spent long hours and tens of thousands of dollars with our attorneys figuring out the right level of disclosure to make to each prospective investor. We didn't want to paint a picture that would scare them away, but we also wanted everyone to feel like they had been fully informed if they chose to invest. We'd send the disclosure papers and hold our breath. Again, as with our previous investors, nobody backed out. It was a time of incredible highs and devastating lows.

But by now, we were growing weary of the treadmill of constantly raising capital and living on the edge. It was stressful and exhausting, and we already had enough stress in our lives. The trouble was that the Waypoint shark was ravenous. Growing and delivering returns to our investors meant that most of the capital we raised went to buying more properties. We were constantly on the verge of running out of operating capital. We needed a huge infusion of capital that would change how Waypoint operated permanently. It was clear that we had only one option going forward.

We would have to do the unthinkable. Waypoint would have to go public.

It was the only way we could get enough capital to keep growing the way our business model demanded. The public markets seemed interested too. Our lawyers, however, were horrified. "You cannot be officers of a public company while you're being investigated by the FBI," they said. Cris warned us against it. We had done nothing wrong, but good defense attorneys are conservative.

But this was a once-in-a-lifetime opportunity. Waypoint was the leader in the SFR industry at this point, but soon larger, richer competitors would come after us. It was now or never, and we had no intention of missing this chance. Against our attorneys' objections, we started building a team. Unfortunately, as we began serious discussions of an IPO in early 2013, it became clear that our attorneys were right. Having us at the wheel of Waypoint as we tried to take the company public would be a mistake. We would have to disclose to every potential underwriter and investor that the two corporate officers might be arrested at any time. Our team felt that to be safe, we would need to disclose everything that was happening to all the different parties that might play a role in our IPO. Public company disclosures are different than in the private sector.

There was no substance to the allegations against us, but going public is difficult under the best of circumstances. Our legal team felt that if we were still running the company, disclosure would wreck our hopes of going public while distracting us from the real task of operating the business. It was incredibly frustrating, but we agreed to step away from our executive roles in the company—essentially, to semiretire. We had built Waypoint from nothing, and now we were having to step aside at a time when we should have been enjoying the ride.

So when we sent our executive team out in early 2013 to do what's called testing the waters—basically, taking meetings with institutional investors to gauge interest in our IPO—we didn't participate. We kept our heads down and let Waypoint's successes speak for themselves. After a while, it looked like we were building a foundation of solid support for a public offering.

## The Article

Then, suddenly, the article came out. On Thursday, March 7, 2013, the news broke in the local press: a huge federal investigation into bid rigging in the Bay Area foreclosure auction market was wrapping up. Unbeknownst to us, the FBI had been investigating bid rigging in the region for years; eventually, they would secure nearly forty guilty pleas. A Department of Justice press release laid it all out:

> Washington—Two Northern California real estate investors have agreed to plead guilty for their role in conspiracies to rig bids and commit mail fraud at public real estate foreclosure auctions in Northern California, the Department of Justice announced.
>
> Felony charges were filed today in the U.S. District Court for the Northern District of California in Oakland against Peter McDonough of Pleasanton, Calif., and Michael Renquist of Livermore, Calif.
>
> Including today's pleas, 29 individuals have pleaded guilty or agreed to plead guilty as a result of the department's ongoing antitrust investigation into bid rigging and fraud at public real estate foreclosure auctions in Northern California.

There was more, but the gist was that the investigation had moved on…and we were not going to be charged! Our attorneys were jubilant. They told us that if federal officials had intended to charge us, they would have at least called us in. For us, the investigation was over. The sense of relief was incredible. This was like having a death sentence commuted at the eleventh hour and *then* getting a full pardon! We could go back to growing Waypoint. Gratefully, we took a collective deep breath, returned to the helm, and started having more serious conversations about going public.

CHAPTER FIVE

# See the Good (and Bad) of Business

In the middle of the fear and chaos surrounding the investigation and our need to raise even more money, we continued to build Waypoint. We didn't do it simply by growing our payroll and our portfolio of rental properties. We also tried to create a company anchored by a clear purpose beyond the act of turning a profit for ourselves and our investors.

In part, this was a matter of survival for us. When we made the decision to go long on our idea, we also committed to working harder and putting in more hours than at any other time in our lives. Scaling a business within a short time horizon is bone crushing. The work becomes your whole life, and on those days when it seems like all you do is put out fires and solve the same problem for the sixth time, one of the only ways you can stay sane and keep yourself moving forward is to have a bigger reason—a bigger "why"—behind your business than just growth and getting rich.

However, while we always tried to do things in what we considered the right way, we were also working in the real world. We encountered our share of fraud, unscrupulous people, and episodes so bizarre that they would have been laughable had they not also been costly. As with the auction misadventure that led to our scary experience with the FBI, although we were trying to be good guys dealing only with good guys, we couldn't seem to avoid tangling with some of the bad guys too.

## It Helps to Know Why You're in Business

Don't get us wrong. We aren't saints. We're not primarily in business out of altruism. We're capitalists, and we like to make money. From 2009 on, we built Waypoint with the help of private individuals who had faith that we would return a substantial profit on their investment. We're big fans of the profit motive, as every entrepreneur in the private sector has to be. However, as we were working what felt like endless hours and taking hair-raising risks with our personal wealth, we knew that we could not allow profit to be the only thing that drove us. We did not want to build something solely to make lots of money. We also wanted to build something with a purpose behind it. We knew we would be working longer and harder than ever before, and at the end of the day when we said, "Why are we doing this?" we wanted the answer to be something more substantial than, "For our bank accounts."

You'll probably find the same thing to be true if you decide to go long on one of your own ideas. The cost of doing it is high, and you'll pay it not only in time at work and away from your family and the activities you enjoy but in stress and worry and frustration and endless assaults on your peace of mind. The way you put up with all that is by knowing that your company is serving a larger cause, maybe by helping people who might otherwise be overlooked or partnering with a nonprofit that does work you care about.

Having a good answer to "Why are we doing this?" matters when you're building a business. Your values matter. Building our company around a larger purpose and the values that meant the most to us helped us put together a team of incredible, dedicated people who worked just as long and hard as we did to make Waypoint a success. We became infamous for having a culture that was intense, demanding, and fast paced; if you didn't fit in or couldn't get the job done, you wouldn't last long. However, in that kind of environment, compensation isn't all that matters to employees. In order to commit to the pace and the intense amount of work, they need to feel like they're part of something that's about helping people and doing good. Authenticity, meaning, and connection help them care about what they do and allow them to show up ready to do it well.

There was more than one purpose behind Waypoint. We wanted to establish SFR as a legitimate asset class by making it more efficient and by making SFR investing and management scalable, and we've done that. But our greater purpose was to help people. We wanted to improve blighted neighborhoods. We wanted to help families who had been through the trauma of foreclosure have places to live that they could take pride in. We wanted to be part of revitalizing communities by increasing the stock of high-quality, affordable rental homes. When we were exhausted after long days of raising money and running the company, we could feel good about what we were doing . . . and why we were doing it.

## Keeping It Real

Part of creating that environment was about us just being our real selves. Joe Maehler, our former Southern California regional director, remembers this well. "Doug and I are very similar and were very competitive with each other," he says. "He's a former pro athlete, and I'm a shorter, fat, White guy, but we would get up in the morning and get our workouts in together. Doug would say, 'Hey, let's get in a run around the lake at six thirty.' So we would run, and Doug would ask an open-ended question, and then he'd push the pace to try to wear you down so he could beat you. You'd have to talk the entire time. Or we'd do pull-up competitions.

"I'd wake up early and answer emails, and that's how I was able to keep up with Doug," Joe continues. "You had to be able to work on his schedule, and you had to be smart enough to get the job done. I think he viewed me as one of his first lieutenants, somebody tough enough to keep the pace who didn't screw stuff up."

What about Colin? "I remember when I started reporting to Colin," Joe recalls. "By that time, I was running all of the investments. We'd had so much success in Southern California that they put me in charge of running acquisitions, and then I ran investments as we started to sell properties. What I would do for Colin is fly around and help guys launch a new region. I would head out there, talk to them, and give them confidence.

"It was fun," Joe goes on. "I reported to Colin when he was

going through his divorce, and during that time, he wrote the single best email I've ever seen in my life. I was working on a big portfolio on a Wednesday afternoon, and he just shot me this email that said, 'I'll be out the next five days. I'm going to Burning Man. And I will be unresponsive.' I thought, *This is the best email I've ever read.* It was the classic midlife crisis email."

Whatever Waypoint was, it was authentic. When he was in the NFL, Doug had the unbelievable experience of playing for a series of iconic coaches: Mike Ditka, Herm Edwards, Tony Dungy, and George Seifert. All of them were different, but the common thread between them was that they were always authentic to who they were. Their values and principles didn't change according to the moment. Tony Dungy could never be Mike Ditka, and Mike Ditka could never be Tony Dungy, but the way they did things was *their* way, and because they were true to their values, their players respected and loved them and would walk into fire for them.

When we came into the SFR market in 2008, we had the freedom to build our company the way we wanted to. We looked at the big REITs and private equity firms who only seemed to care about the bottom line instead of people and said, "That's not who we're going to be." We decided we would follow our own guiding star in SFR and build a company that was about more than just turning a profit. With any business, a key metric of success is sustainability. Can you build something and then keep it going and thriving for the long haul? We believe you can, and we also believe it's easier when you and your team are pulling together to serve something more than the bottom line.

## The Stanford Business Case

In April 2013, the Stanford Graduate School of Business published a business case on Waypoint. Written by David Hoyt and George Foster, the publication was an enormous honor for us and recognition of what we were doing by some of the sharpest minds in all of the business world.

Stanford's business case studies highlight companies and ideas that the authors and the university feel represent important inflection points in their industries—moments of change, vital innovations, or calls to action that they feel can be instructive to business students and the larger academic community. In 2020, Stanford business cases leaned heavily toward artificial intelligence but also looked at individual entrepreneurs, companies, and sectors, such as digital banking in the Middle East.

Our business case was called "Waypoint: Reinventing Single Family Home Rental," and apart from telling the Waypoint origin story in granular detail, it talked about some of the dynamics of the company and the choices we made—to recruit people who were outside the SFR industry, to publicize our fundraising deal with GI Partners even though it meant attracting the attention of competitors, our dedication to twenty-four seven customer service, and so on. It broke down our Compass technology platform and laid out the rationale for our eventual expansion into Southern California, Chicago, Atlanta, Phoenix, Florida, and beyond.

The authors also captured a terrific quote from Gary Beasley that perfectly reflects Waypoint's larger purpose and our belief that doing business based in part on values and conscience helped us succeed:

> Ironically, I think [the social benefit] is one of the things that has helped us financially, because it has helped build a reputation that is based on genuine beliefs and action, that the business is thinking about things the right way, and is treating people with respect and is out to help rebuild communities. Of course, we're out to do well financially, but we're doing so in a way that is sensitive to the communities and to the people we're interacting with.

The Stanford publication documented what we had known since the start, which was that the Waypoint business model, while it seemed like a shot in the dark in 2008, was actually based on sound real estate market data and strong financial metrics, especially when it came to calculating ROI. It was incredibly validating to know that our methodology would be used to teach business students how to think and act like entrepreneurs both within and outside the real estate space.

## Adding More Great People

Another highlight of this era at Waypoint was that we were able to keep building our team with some of the best people in the real estate world. For some reason, there was a kind of magic at work with us, because great people just seemed to come out of the woodwork and join the team. We worked hard, but we had a lot of fun together too, and as we onboarded one new group of great people, other potential hires were watching. They saw what a great culture we had. Recruitment and retention, giant headaches for many organizations, were not a problem for us.

It went like this: someone would hear about Waypoint, we'd

bring them in, they would meet the other people on the team, and inevitably they would tell us, "This is the most high-caliber group I've ever worked with." They were in. In a way, our most important skill set wasn't actually building business models or designing technology solutions. It was creating an exciting, compelling vision and then selling people on it. That's what we did with our investors, and it's what we did in hiring.

Some of our employees actually turned down more money to work for us. When we asked them why, they said that we had a more compelling vision and a more impressive track record. They also thought that we were the good guys. One told us, "You guys seem more real. The private equity companies are like traveling salesmen—they make up a bunch of stuff. You guys are telling us what's wrong with the business."

Mike Travalini was one of them. Mike stalked Doug to get a job with Waypoint. He was working for an apartment company called Larimar, buying small apartment buildings. He saw the foreclosure crisis coming, thought it was a huge opportunity, wrote a white paper on buying single-family rentals, and presented it to Larimar, which shot it down. So Mike did some research, found Waypoint, realized that he and Doug had a connection, called him, and within fifteen minutes they had a meeting scheduled. The next week, Mike showed up in Oakland and slapped down his white paper showing how single-family rentals could be turned into an asset class and expanded into multiple markets. We hired him. How could we not? He helped us expand into new markets, and then he ran Chicago for us.

When we started having problems with repairs and maintenance on our portfolio of homes, Mike really showed his value. Maintenance issues can be a disaster with a nationwide network of properties if you don't get them under control. Mike is a subject matter expert in repairs and maintenance because he spent so many years in multifamily real estate. When we were struggling to create efficiency in providing repairs and maintenance, we asked him to leave operations and run repairs and maintenance, which no one had ever run as a separate department. He thought it was a crazy idea, but he ended up turning the situation around and really saved the day. He went on to be president of SMS Assist, a national tech-enabled repair and maintenance service, and as we write this, he's launching a virtual R&M start-up. By stepping into a new and difficult position for Waypoint and performing brilliantly, he changed his whole career trajectory.

We asked Mike to tell us some of his favorite Waypoint stories, which was easy because Mike likes to talk. A lot. We just asked a question, then sat back and let the recorder run. "Frankly, it was, hands down, the best career experience I ever had," Mike says. "The team that we built, with everybody going on the same mission, was the most exciting place that I've worked—the most exciting mission I've been a part of."

Mike's a Chicago guy, and he wanted to convince Doug to take Waypoint to Chicago with Mike at the helm. The persistence, plus Mike's skills and talent, paid off. "I had already given notice at my job when I got this call from Doug. I think he was on a YPO retreat," Mike says. "I said, 'You know what, Doug? I really hope to convince you to do this in Chicago, and I want to do it with you. But I've decided that if I can't do it with you, I'm going to do it myself anyway.' Doug was blown away. I had an offer letter within twenty-four hours of that conversation.

"However, Doug said later, 'You've done enough to convince me that you understand real estate investing. So I actually don't want you to work in Chicago. I want you to help me open all of our new locations.' Here I am, maybe thirty-two years old, and I'm so psyched that this guy believes in me enough to give me a try, working alone from my dining room in Chicago. After that, there was no turning back."

Mike was another of the core gang who just vibed with each other. We worked incredibly hard, fought, butted heads, and had an incredible time building this company. We had real chemistry, which makes those long hours and late nights a lot easier to take. "There was so much camaraderie on the team," Mike says. "Doug and Colin would host off-sites and get people together. I used to give Doug a lot of shit, because we would have our weekly or biweekly one-on-one and he would dive right in: 'Hey, Trav, here are the ten things on my list that I need answers from you on.' When I got to know Doug better, I would just say, 'You know, Doug, it'd be really nice if you would just pretend for two minutes that you care about anything besides your sacred Google Doc.'

"What I wanted was for him to share the document with me, let me look at it myself, and prepare for the meeting rather than him run through a task list and not give me the professional discretion to manage my own business," Mike goes on. "I poked a lot of fun at Doug, and he took it really well. He was adaptable. He listened and he cared, but his way of showing it was just very different than anyone's I had ever worked with.

"It was intense to figure out Doug's style and figure out how to make it work, but he made me grow up really fast," Mike continues. "Now I look back and appreciate how much he helped me grow professionally. His style, while super intense for the guys who could survive it, was a big reason the business succeeded. Doug would never let it fail."

As often happens, this special team broke up after Waypoint merged with Starwood Capital (which we'll talk about shortly), but like so many others who were there in the trenches beside us, Mike remembers Waypoint fondly. "I loved it. I love those guys," he says. "Not quite a year, probably nine months after the merger, Doug and Colin hosted this sort of celebratory reunion at a vineyard in Napa and had a bunch of the executives come back and get together for dinner. It reminded me of how much I loved the team and the environment. It was like we had never left each other. I remember how bittersweet that was.

"I made these friends, many of whom I still talk to. The core five of us, we talk frequently. I check in with Doug and Ali pretty regularly. Waypoint is something that I will look back on fondly for the rest of my life. I was part of something that I truly believed in. I would have jumped through any hoops that I needed to make our business successful. At the same time, it helped me grow into an adult professional—probably gave me the equivalent of ten or twenty years of career experience in just four."

David Zanaty was another member of that core group. David was our regional director for Atlanta. We liked starting talented people out as regional directors. They owned their market in terms of setup, growth, building local infrastructure, hiring, and being the center of the corporate culture. It was a great way to see who could lead, and David had the stuff. He's very polished, a real CEO type. He's from Atlanta, so he started and ran the Atlanta market for us, and we ultimately promoted him to run the entire Eastern region. After he left, he worked for some big developers but told us that after Waypoint, he could never go back and just do traditional real estate. After he did a stint at tech-powered residential sales company Opendoor, we hired him for Mynd. We love the idea of getting the Waypoint band back together.

When we talked to David, he also had a lot to say about the demanding Waypoint culture. "There was a level of intensity and urgency," he says. "We were out running. We were trying to outrun the clock and our competitors too. We didn't know when the market would recover and close the buying window. We didn't know when a competitor would come along and change pricing. So we were trying to move really fast.

"One other interesting dynamic I was exposed to that I really hadn't seen before was radical candor," David continues. "We didn't call it that. We certainly didn't circulate the book at that point, as I did in later chapters in my career. But giving and receiving difficult feedback led to massive personal growth for all of us. It was only possible because we knew that we cared about each other. It was a neat element, to know that we could be direct with each other and challenge each other up, down, and across the organization, with our teams or with each other, and know that we were trying to get better."

Getting better was critical to us at Waypoint. We knew we had built an astonishing team, and we wanted everyone to keep improving. "Through coaching, off-sites, and feedback, there were lots of opportunities to stretch, and it changed the trajectory for a lot of us in terms of what we thought was possible in our career and what we're capable of today," David goes on. "I left in February of 2016, so I've been gone longer than I was there, but it's almost like college in the sense that those four years are really important. We're all still in touch. It's like no time has passed in some respects. There was a lot of urgency, but the bond lets you survive the urgency. If a team is bonding the way we did, it's not work. The bond allows urgency to become a kind of force multiplier or an accelerant. The team becomes a brotherhood—and I hesitate to use that word because there were females involved as well. The team was rooted in the idea that, 'I'm not going to be the one to underperform. I'm not going to let the team down.' The exceptional effort that was required was enabled by the bond."

Another key piece in that team puzzle was Rich Rodriguez, a former Navy SEAL who came on board in 2013 as our senior VP of operations and is now executive vice president and head of real estate operations at Amherst Residential. Doug got his name from George Casey, a residential builder guru who was one of the early pioneers to see the SFR opportunity and had George make an introduction. We liked talented people and knew that as a former SEAL, Rich could more than handle Waypoint's "leave it all on the court" approach to growth.

"I think one of the keys to their being able to do what they did was they were willing to play big when everybody else was playing small," Rich says. "Back in 2008 and 2009, it was mostly flippers flipping a couple of properties at a time. But Doug and Colin had this idea to buy up hundreds. Of course, it became tens of thousands of properties. We were at maybe the seven thousand mark when I joined.

"But I did my own research after the call," Rich continues. "I may have acted like I knew what they were talking about, but I made a lot of calls afterward. What were these guys talking about? What is this thing called SFR? I reached out to George Casey, and he said, 'This is the future. I've been talking about this for years, and these guys are smart. They've got a vision, and you should latch on to them.' We were disciplined. We had a plan. We took regular business metrics and incorporated them into SFR—basic things like cycle time, budget, variance, quality measures, all those things that you need to be a top-tier operator in any business. It's not just about churning out the volume.

"We were higher quality. We had better processes. I think the financials bore that out as well. We were just saying, 'We're going to be better than those guys.' So there was some ego there too."

Rich is a highly decorated former captain in the Navy SEALs who, after thirty-three years, still serves as reserve vice director for Joint Force Development and holds the rank of rear admiral. So not only did he experience the competitive side of Waypoint, but he contributed to it too, as he relates: "Just after I joined the company, we did an off-site in Phoenix. I've got a military background, and I was still in the reserves," Rich says. "So, in the morning, I put the senior team through a workout. Me being new to the company, I figured, *Okay, I'm just gonna crush these guys.* Around the hotel, I set up eight stations, and they had to run about an eighth of a mile between stations and do a series of exercises at each one. It took about an hour and a half to do this. I crushed them.

"Doug couldn't make the thing," Rich goes on. "Finally, he comes jogging out to visit, and we had just finished the workout. I looked at him, and he looked at me, and I'm like, 'All right, let's do it again.' So we did it again, this time with Doug. I did it again, and the other guys all did it twice too. Another time Doug convinced me, Joe Maehler, and one other guy to go do the Spartan Beast obstacle course race, a half-marathon up in Sacramento. Doug crushed everybody, including me."

That was Waypoint in those early days. Extreme, competitive, and maybe just a little bit sadistic. But we sure did some great business and had a lot of fun along the way.

## The Human Toll of the Recession

While all that was happening, regular people were suffering. From the beginning, one of the core values of Waypoint was that behind every one of those vacant East Bay properties we saw as we drove around for our initial research was a real family that was losing its home. That knowledge kept us grounded and focused on our values. We always tried to remember that real estate is about people, not just houses.

It's been more than twelve years since the financial collapse and the Great Recession, so it's easy to forget just how bad things were and how terrifying life was for the majority of Americans who lived paycheck to paycheck. Here's a little refresher course.

Between 2007 and 2009, unemployment spiked to 10 percent. Americans saw $9.8 trillion in wealth evaporate, much of it from home values and retirement accounts, which took on water as global stock markets tumbled. Contrast this with the economic collapse that ensued when the COVID-19 pandemic shut down much of the US economy in 2020 and 2021. Those months were brutal, but the fundamentals of the economy were strong, and as we write this, most economists expect the economy to stage a pretty robust recovery once the pandemic is under control. However, in 2008, the fundamentals had been shattered by the incredible amount of leverage taken on by lenders, investment banks, investors, and regular homeowners. Bouncing back took the better part of a decade, and it left a lot of people far worse off than they had been.

The scars of that time run deep. Many people have still not recovered financially, and some never will. The Federal Reserve Bank of St. Louis found that in 2018, the average net worth of a family led by a twenty-four-year-old millennial was about

$5,072. For the family of a forty-eight-year-old, that average was $130,454. Many millennials began their careers at a time when opportunity and earning power were at historic lows, and some of them will never claw back that lost ground. COVID-19 has only made the problem worse.

Many people who lost good jobs in 2008 have had a hard time finding new jobs that pay as well. The Federal Reserve Bank of San Francisco has estimated that the Great Recession will cost the average American $70,000 in lifetime earnings. Also, according to ATTOM Data Solutions, one in ten American homes is still at least 25 percent underwater, where the owner owes more on the house than its market value. Finally, the recession crushed rural economies. And that was all before the pandemic sucker punched the US again.

## A Path Back to Homeownership

All this is by way of saying that when we started hunting around the East Bay for undervalued homes, we were mindful that we were driving around ground zero of a personal disaster. Families were being evicted and foreclosed upon left and right. Neighborhoods were empty and desolate. Driving down the streets was surreal sometimes. Once those vacant houses became dilapidated, where would people live? A fog of fear hung over everything. Because of that, we had a dual focus in the earliest days of Waypoint. Yes, we wanted to acquire a lot of homes, rent them, and watch them appreciate, but we also wanted to create a path back to homeownership for people who had been victims of this crisis.

We decided to create a business model that would appease our investors while attracting the best kind of renters—renters who wanted to be owners. Doing this was in our best interest; renters who want to buy are far more likely than other groups of renters to pay their rent on time and to take care of their homes, which in turn lowers our maintenance costs and enhances the eventual resale value of the property. We were trying to create a win-win, and that reputation helped us attract both renters and great employees. We would not be predators. We would be part of the solution.

By focusing on the human factor, we added dimensions of purpose and meaning to what we were doing. We had a mission to help people, and that motivated us not only as businessmen and investors but as human beings. It was a powerful burnout preventer. The long hours, endless fundraising, and constant push to scale Waypoint might have become too much if we had been in it just for the money. The thrill of entrepreneurship starts to pale when you haven't had a full night's sleep in six months. Making your business into something that matters helps you keep charging forward.

Many successful entrepreneurs understand this philosophy. Logan Allec, owner of Money Done Right, told *Business News Daily*, "Entrepreneurship is, fundamentally, the art and science of building profitable systems to help people in ways that other systems do not. The core competency of the entrepreneur is not business acumen or marketing ability but rather empathy—the ability to understand the feelings and needs of others."

In the same publication, Konrad Billetz, cofounder and co-CEO of Offset Solar, said, "Entrepreneurship is the ability to recognize the bigger picture, find where there's an opportunity to make someone's life better, design hypotheses around these opportunities and continually test your assumptions. It's experimentation: Some experiments will work; many others will fail. It is not big exits, huge net worth or living a life of glamour. It's hard work and persistence to leave the world a better place once your time here is done."

## Lease Purchase

We had that larger purpose—a path back to homeownership for folks who had been displaced by a financial disaster they had no part in creating—in mind when we started our lease-purchase option program in the middle of 2009.

When we were out scouting homes in the early days of the collapse, we witnessed the devastation, and it really affected us. Deserted streets, overgrown yards, empty schools, boarded-up windows, overflowing mailboxes, vandalism, and scrawled messages on walls filled with anguish, frustration, and anger. It was heartbreaking.

Most of the people who had left those homes behind were not deadbeats. They were victims of a system that preyed on their hunger to own a home by offering them booby-trapped mortgages while telling them everything was going to be all right. The majority of them were guilty of nothing but believing the fairy tales their mortgage brokers and real estate agents had fed them about ever-rising home prices. They hadn't bought the credit default swaps and collateralized debt obligations that brought down the economy. They'd just signed where they were told to sign. If we could help them rebuild their lives while scoring terrific renters who would help us be more profitable, why wouldn't we do that?

Our lease-purchase option (LPO) was structured so that each month the resident would pay a small option fee on top of their rent that would accrue toward helping them buy the house at a later date. The resident would have the option—but not the obligation—to buy the house in the future. If they chose to exercise their option and buy, Waypoint would be obligated to sell it to them at their predetermined price.

The idea was that over time, our residents would save money they could apply toward the purchase of a house they were already living in, improve their credit by reliably paying their rent, and in a few years become homeowners again. We even offered residents professional financial counseling, and we created a system called Waypoints, in which residents who paid their rent on time, passed inspections, and met a few other requirements could accrue points they could use for discounts on later rent increases, televisions, and so on. It sounded great.

Reality, however, was a little trickier. Because the LPO was structured to allow the resident to eventually buy their house at an agreed-upon price that was higher than the home's value when they moved in, the whole thing depended on East Bay property values going up. The problem was, for a while in 2009, prices continued going down. Meanwhile, the purchase price for the home remained the same. Some renters were paying option money every month for houses that were underwater, meaning they would have to wait until housing prices turned around in order to be able to finance a purchase.

After a while, some folks in the LPO program became angry and accused us of running a scam. Some even vandalized their houses to get back at us. It was an unfortunate turn of events, a confluence of stagnant prices and impatient renters desperate to get back to being homeowners again. We had explained carefully that while the area's real estate prices might continue to fall for a little while, they were certain to rise considerably over time. All they needed was some patience. We put everything in writing and thought we had given them peace of mind, but some of our residents just didn't understand the risks. Sometimes when you're an entrepreneur, things don't work out despite your best intentions.

Around the end of 2010, we reluctantly shut the LPO program down. The misunderstanding with our renters was one reason; investor feedback was another. We couldn't control our exit timing or price, which was a big issue for investors. At that point, we had no choice but to kill the program. Our intentions had been good, but you know what is said to be paved with good intentions. Still, everyone felt good about what we had tried to do.

The LPO program wasn't without a few wins. For one thing, the people who stayed in the program and held on to their houses got incredible deals three or four years later when prices went through the roof. We were handing over the title papers on homes purchased at $185,000 when the market value of the house might be $40,000 higher. It felt really good to help some people own homes again. But our best lease-option story is about Darren Gates and his family.

## Darren Gates

Darren's house marked the first time we bought a foreclosure house that the family was still living in. This was actually part of our LPO model. We wanted to buy houses with the owners still living in them and then say, "Do you want to stay in your house? Here's a way to buy your house back." We figured that these people loved these houses, so they would take good care of them and be terrific renters, and we were right. It also felt really good to give people a chance to stay in their homes. There's a deep sense of shame, failure, and betrayal attached to being foreclosed upon; that's one reason many people react with rage and violence. But when we approached former owners with our proposal, they usually ended up hugging us and crying, relieved that we were giving them a chance to get their house—and their dignity—back.

We bought Darren's house at an auction in Antioch, and of course we didn't know what the inside of the house looked like, so we decided to drive over to have a look. When we got out of the car and walked up the front walk, we saw a woman in the kitchen window watching us like we were the Grim Reaper. She knew exactly what was going on. We have never felt more self-conscious in our lives than we did that day, walking up those steps to tell those people that we had just bought their house. We had every legal right to be there, but it was excruciating.

We knocked, and Darren answered the door. He knew too. We could see it in his eyes. He was expecting the axe to fall and probably hoping that he wouldn't have to cry or beg in front of his four kids. Darren was a contractor whose business had collapsed after the bottom fell out of the real estate market—a solid, hardworking guy, just another victim of fraud and recklessness and economic forces beyond his control.

Every now and then the world presents you with an opportunity to be of service—to change someone's life for the better—and this was one of them. We introduced ourselves, sat down with the couple, and told them about our lease-option program. The change in their faces was incredible; in a split-second, they went from fear and dread to surprise and hope. We gave them the details of the lease-purchase option program, and they were totally on board.

It changed their lives. First, they thought they were losing their house. Not only did they sign onto the LPO program and stay in the house as renters, but Darren ended up working for Waypoint. He was a top-notch contractor, and at that time, we were looking for contractors to handle our renovation work. We hired him, and after a while, his whole business was Waypoint. He was renovating ten to twenty houses a month for us, so he started making great money. After three or four years, he bought his house back at a great price. He even did a big renovation on Doug's home that won a design award from the city of Piedmont.

That's one of the few feel-good stories to come out of that dark time, and our only regret is that the market didn't let us do the same for more people. But we did make life better for people like Darren, and that's not a bad day's work.

## The Seven Deadly CFOs

We also had our share of misadventures along the way, especially with our financials. When things got ugly, Nina Tran saved us when no one else could.

One of our biggest early mistakes in building Waypoint was that we failed to hire a good CFO. We didn't even have a really good accountant on board. There's a breaking-news story for you: *get the accounting right*. You heard it here first. We struggled to get our accounting in order. It was a nightmare.

Part of the problem was that every house we bought had its own set of books, and there were thousands of houses in our real estate portfolio. We also had our allocation methodology, which meant we had to track how much we spent on renovations, construction management, and acquisitions, divided by the number of houses in each phase of an operation during a given period of time. The bookkeeping was very complicated, and documenting and truing up every transaction was tedious and time consuming.

Also, remember that in order to fund Waypoint in its early days, we had raised multiple funds from private investors: five funds in total. Each fund bought its own specific group of houses. Because of that, the company's books were crisscrossed with intrafund loans. One fund would lend money to another fund as needed. For example, there might be an expense that several funds shared, so one fund would lend the others the money to cover that expense, and the other funds would reimburse the paying fund when rent came in. It was all completely aboveboard and legal, but we had to keep track of which funds had made loans to which other funds during which periods and which allocations had gone to the houses in what phase. The result was a labyrinth of accounting documentation that had to be untangled like fishing line. Our problem was that we couldn't find anyone who would invest the time to trace and reconcile every transaction.

Thus began our own version of the movie *Groundhog Day*, except that in our case, we kept having the same experiences with chief financial officers over and over again. Waypoint went through seven CFOs or top accountants—you can call them the Seven Deadly CFOs, because six of them were deadly to our peace of mind and future ability to go public. The first was Jeff. One day Jeff told us that the books were a mess, could not be saved, and that he was quitting. Another CFO du jour (whose name we've erased from our minds for our own protection) sat us down and explained that Waypoint Real Estate Group owed itself $1.5 million.

It took us a minute before we said, "Excuse me?"

The soon-to-be-ex-CFO repeated himself.

"How could that even happen?" we asked.

His reply: "I don't know." Word of advice for CFOs: if you're going to tell your employer that they owe themselves seven figures due to some combination of recklessness and carelessness, be sure you're ready with a better answer than "I don't know."

On another occasion, we discovered that because of accounting incompetence, fund three, which had already distributed its returns to investors, owed Waypoint $300,000. Uh, thanks, but we're going to eat that deficit for the time being. Can you imagine us going back to our fund three investors, hat in hand, and saying something like, "We're very sorry, but we're going to need you to return $300,000 of that money we just gave you, please"? No. Instead, we lived with that situation for several years before Nina helped clean up the mess.

Then there was the time that our sixth CFO accused us of running a Ponzi scheme. He didn't understand the nature of our multiple funds, so he came to us one day and said, "I think there's a Ponzi scheme happening here. You guys are taking from one fund to fund another fund." He didn't understand that in real estate funds, intercompany loans are very common. To him, that meant they were unethical. Needless to say, he didn't solve our accounting issues, and he didn't stay an employee of Waypoint very long, either.

That's how it was with each CFO or accountant we hired. The cycle repeated with a ghastly predictability. New financial professionals would come in, look at our tangle of transactions and records, have small panic attacks, and then roll up their sleeves and try to make some sense of it all. Unfortunately, after a time, they would either give up in frustration and resign or make an even bigger mess of things.

We were just as frustrated. We had followed generally accepted accounting practices. There wasn't anything unconventional or suspicious in our books. We knew a solution was a matter of finding someone with the right expertise who would put in the work. We just couldn't find that person. We needed help—and quickly. Our business was becoming more complex by the year, and we were concerned that accounting oversights might leave us with a huge and unexpected financial liability at a time when we were dealing with the FBI and thinking about going public. We needed to know precisely where we were financially.

Then came CFO number seven, Nina Tran. Nina was our savior. She was deadly—not to our business, but to chaos. We brought her in because we were thinking about taking the company public, and if we were to do that, our books had to be spotless. Nina came in and said, "I've got this," and she did. She was the first financial professional who told us that our financial structure was perfectly normal—the transactions just needed to be traced.

When she took the job, we realized that our books weren't the problem. Our previous financial officers had either been not good enough or too lazy to figure things out. Nina was persevering, incredibly detail oriented, and relentless. She had a twenty-year résumé and been the head of accounting for a large public corporation, so she was a completely different caliber of financial professional.

She and her team rolled up their sleeves. The work was time consuming, but they followed every transaction from beginning to end to make sure that it was 100 percent trued up in a verifiable way. Nina also put together an organizational plan for us, and within a few weeks, our accounting problems were untangled. The clouds parted, and the sun shone. We had to cut a check for about $150,000 to clean up loans that couldn't be clearly traced, and after that, everything was in order. Nina was the quiet superhero of Waypoint.

"Prior to me joining as CFO, they had gone through three CFOs in two years," Nina says. "But for me, it was a lot of cleaning up and getting the team right, hiring the right talent to get us prepared to go public. What really made Waypoint so special was the dynamic of the core leaders, who brought us from a small entrepreneurial company that didn't have a lot of process and structure to a more grown-up company that was able to go public and do serious institutional investing.

"It was that fast pace with a lot of really smart, motivated individuals, which made it really special," Nina continues. "And it was fun as well. I headed up the culture committee. We had the Waypoint Olympics, where we would split employees into different teams by different levels and departments. And we would compete with one another in things like chair curling, Nerf gun shooting, triathlon, basketball shooting with papers, things like that. It brought the company together. People would buy T-shirts for their team, paint their faces, and come up with names and so forth. It made the culture really fun."

## California Scheming

Sadly, balancing out all the wonderful people like Darren and Nina were a small army of fraudsters. Long before COVID-19, the foreclosure crisis unleashed a plague of fraud: bid rigging, unqualified contractors ripping off homeowners, real estate agents and mortgage brokers falsifying documents, and a lot more.

During the Great Recession, spammers would send people emails claiming that then-President Obama was giving out checks. Scammers would entice people to invest their money in fake CDs, fake investments in gold and silver, private real estate deals for properties that didn't exist or that they didn't own, and all manner of other schemes. Many of them turned out to be Ponzi schemes, while others were just theft. Times of chaos and fear always bring out the fraudsters, and Waypoint was not immune.

We had launched our Southern California division with high hopes that we could make inroads in one of the most desirable rental markets in the country. But before too long, we became aware that there was some shady stuff going on with one of our regional directors, whom we'll call Steve (not his real name).

We assigned a member of our team, Andrew, to travel to the region to investigate. He got back to us with a deeply disturbing report. He had gotten a look at Steve's laptop (which was Waypoint property) and found evidence of behavior that wasn't just sketchy. It was immoral and illegal and put Waypoint at a lot of risk. This was the conversation Doug had about what Andrew found:

> *Andrew: Doug, we have an issue here.*
> *Doug: What do you mean?*
> *Andrew: There were some compromising photos of Steve.*
> *Doug: What do you mean, compromising?*
> *Andrew: Inappropriate.*
> *Doug: What do you mean, inappropriate?*
> *Andrew: He had pictures of his genitals on his laptop. Also, there were suggestive emails.*
> *Doug: Really? Can you be more specific?*

> *Andrew: Loony emails, completely inappropriate.*
>
> *Doug: How inappropriate?*
>
> *Andrew: He was screwing our realtor on the kitchen counter in one of our houses. Is that enough detail?*
>
> *Doug: Well, that's not good.*

There was more. Apparently, Steve was not only having a romantic interlude with this realtor and drinking in the office, he had apparently passed out at his desk one day and one of our other employees found him. Worst of all, he and his paramour were running a fraud scheme. When they bought a house, they would report a higher price to us than they were actually paying. They were skimming the difference and using those funds to buy wholesale properties for themselves, which they would then flip.

I guess they thought we were as dumb as they were. After all, our model was precise; it told us exactly what we should pay for any house in any market. So after a little while, we started asking, "Why are we paying so much for houses in this market?" The numbers weren't adding up. That was the red flag, and when we figured out what was going on, we naturally fired Steve.

We had another regional director—this time in Tampa, Florida—who we suspected was defrauding Waypoint at a much larger scale than Steve. Best we could figure it, he had arrangements with all these different contractors who would charge us about 20 percent more for the work they did than the work actually cost. Of course, they would then kick most of that money back to the regional director. But we needed proof, so we dealt with that in a way that was more . . . creative.

We told Rich Rodriguez (who, remember, was a Navy SEAL), "We need you to go out to Tampa undercover. Nobody can know you're there, or they'll get super suspicious. We need you to literally go through all these houses that we renovated, get the paperwork, and do an audit. We need you to be like a commando—a Navy SEAL! Nobody sees you. If they do, they have to die."

Obviously, we weren't serious about the last part, but we did need Rich to stage a sort of covert op. He would take four or five days, go through every renovated house, and find the ones where the dollars we were billed didn't match the dollars spent. We already knew things didn't add up, but we needed more details.

Well, it was like a scene out of *Goodfellas*. After Rich did his recon flawlessly, Joe Maehler and Doug flew out and met him at this shady little restaurant off the beaten path and put all their notes together. When they decided they had enough evidence, they went over to the office. But they went in military style, locked everybody in the office, and separated them so they couldn't get their stories straight. They scared them by talking about how the Tampa police would be arriving in three hours, and if they didn't get straight answers, Waypoint would press charges. Everybody started ratting each other out, and we found out that we were getting robbed blind in Tampa.

The entire Tampa team was in on the scheme. They would collect revenue for renovations that weren't done. They would buy a property for less than they reported to us and would pocket the difference. In the end, we didn't have enough evidence to prove that crimes had occurred, and we didn't have the time to gather it. So we fired everyone on the spot and just moved on.

That's why we laugh when we hear about companies moving their headquarters to Florida to avoid taxes. We had such a hard time finding quality talent to build around. It's not that there aren't talented people in Florida, but it's not the Bay Area.

As we learned, fast growth comes with its own risks. In the real estate market at that time, everyone was looking for an angle and trying to make a buck. There were no rules. Because we were deploying so much capital so quickly, we were highly vulnerable to fraud. To stop the flow of losses due to fraud, we had to put all sorts of protocols in place. Eventually, twice a year we had our employees fill out a questionnaire to confirm that they were not engaged in practices that could create opportunities for fraud, such as having business dealings with friends or relatives.

However, there was a lot more good than sketchy at Waypoint, even in those days, as Charles Young points out. "Long term, values are what help you build a culture that lasts and a company that's going to last," he says. "A lot of that is still in our current culture at Invitation Homes. I'm still here four mergers later, but I can sit at my desk here in Dallas and still see a Waypoint values sign on my wall. That's what you do. Bring your A game, rally the team, do the right thing, manage them well, and be the solution. Those were the Waypoint values, and I still keep them in our business today."

## CHAPTER SIX

# Race a Sailboat

By early 2013, values, nerve, and a lot of work had turned Waypoint into a growth machine and probably the leading investment firm in the SFR space. After two-and-a-half years, the FBI episode was finally behind us. We had the funds from Citibank in the bank, and we were back to doing what we did best—aggressively buying and managing properties.

But even with that big capital infusion, we knew that eventually we would face another high-pressure round of raising money, which meant more endless negotiations with private equity investors and banks. No thank you. Constantly begging for capital was not only exhausting, it left us little time to run our company, which was what we enjoyed. It was clearly time for us to take Waypoint public.

This was consistent with a strategy some people refer to as

"sailboat racing." If you've ever watched a sailboat race like the America's Cup, you probably noticed that most of the time the boat that gets out to an early lead is the same boat that wins the race. All the boats are using the same wind, so once one boat is firmly in the lead, all the trailing vessels can do is make small adjustments to the sail trim and steering to gain a few fractions of a knot. But unless the leader has a mechanical breakdown or makes a terrible tactical error, the race is usually over. The point is, when you have the chance to take a lead, take it.

In business, the sailboat race principle is similar. When you're in the early stages of a business with a high potential upside, do everything you can to scale and gain market share, even at the expense of profitability. The beginning is the time to build your big lead because early on most of the big players will probably be ignoring you or expecting you to fail. They won't be direct competitors yet.

Sooner or later, that will change. You're providing your competitors with real-time market research. When you've proved that your business model is sound and that there are substantial profits to be made in your market, other boats will get on the water, and they might be bigger and faster than yours. Competitors will outspend you, "borrow" your ideas, and try to crush you. If you have a large lead on them, you may be able to stay alive and formulate a strategy, whether that means going public, selling your company, or merging with one of your adversaries. If not, they will either drive you out of business or capture so much market share that you'll never be more than a fringe player.

With Waypoint, we faced exactly that situation. Back in 2008, we looked at the SFR data and the financials and saw that we were the only sailors on a sea of profit. So we decided to go big. We pounced on the opportunity. We sacrificed our family time. We risked most of our personal wealth. We worked harder than we had ever worked before. We wanted to get our sailboat way out in front of the pack because we knew that sooner or later slow-moving but well-funded competitors would catch on to what we were doing and come gunning for us. We wanted to have a substantial lead when they did. Going public would be our big gun in taking a lead we hoped would be insurmountable.

## Expansion

This drive to build a huge lead in SFR was why, during the previous year—even with the prospect of felony charges looming over us—we had been raising funds, buying houses, and hiring. We'd even made the decision to expand beyond the Bay Area. We hired a team of regional managers who went into other metro areas to scout single-family home inventory, get our data gathering and automated underwriting up and running, make offers, and close on houses. This was critical because the Bay Area was becoming crowded with well-funded competitors who were raising prices and increasing the competition for the best homes. Expansion into markets that were less picked over was a necessity if we wanted to continue scaling the company. Eventually, we would be in thirteen markets nationwide.

Of course, when you get out of familiar territory, you find out how well your systems work because you can't manage everything personally. You're exporting a turnkey solution and hoping someone else can make it go. Our system for locating, underwriting, bidding on, buying, and renovating homes worked well in our other markets, but there were also some holes in the system. Every state and city has its own way of doing business. The rules governing real estate brokers are different, deals often flow differently, and city-specific building codes can affect renovation. Plus, the optimal neighborhoods for undervalued homes are *very* different.

Our regional managers had to get boots on the ground and set everything up from scratch. Mistakes were made. But overall, the systems we created in the Bay Area worked pretty well when we exported them to other metro areas. An undervalued house in a promising neighborhood was essentially the same in Antioch as it was in Atlanta or Los Angeles. By early 2013, we had more than four hundred employees scattered across the country and were collecting annual rents totaling about $125 million.

Earlier we mentioned Joe Maehler, our first regional director for Southern California and one of the core leaders of Waypoint. Joe is an entrepreneurial, hardworking, scrappy guy, and when he jumped into the LA real estate market, he built our infrastructure there—contractors, brokers, lenders, field personnel—from the ground up. He proved our model could work elsewhere and ended up becoming our VP of acquisitions. Joe was always a great ambassador for the Waypoint ethos: always on the road talking to everyone in different offices, helping to instill the right culture and values.

But joining Waypoint wasn't all smooth sailing for Joe. "On MLK Day of 2011, Bob, my former partner, and I were out touring the market, and I got an email: Doug and Colin had gotten a subpoena from the FBI for collusion on the courthouse steps. We finished our tour and went back to the office. Doug called us and said, 'Look, we've got to let you guys go.' I'd never been fired from a job in my life. We're like, 'Dude, we shut down a business that was going well to take this huge entrepreneurial risk, and you fire us within a month?'

"Bob and I talked for an hour: 'What are you going to do? I don't know, what are *you* going to do?'" Joe continues. "My thought was to just go and get hammered. Then the next day, Tuesday morning, we talked some more, and we just figured the opportunity was too big to pass up. So we kept going and worked for ourselves. Within three weeks, Doug hired us back."

Good thing too. Joe was everything we wanted from a regional director: smart, creative, with lots of integrity. He needed all those assets because Southern California is a challenge. "Being a regional director was a badge of honor for a couple of reasons," Joe says. "One, you basically had to run your own business. Two, Waypoint was the intersection of tech and real estate, and nobody knew what they were doing yet. You had to have a lot of business acumen to take pressure from three angles.

"First, there was the tech department, trying to force you to use automation and systems that were homogenous across the entire platform when real estate is completely different in different markets," Joe goes on. "You're also hiring the vast majority of your employees—lower-wage employees—yourself. Three, there was intense pressure from the home office, especially from Doug. I had those three pressure points pushing on everything, and this is the perfect example of how that worked out."

Joe also learned that while you could build all sorts of cool technology, getting people to use it was a little more challenging. "We were developing all these apps our construction guys could use to go around and figure out the punch list for a property so they could determine how much it would cost to renovate," he says. "They would try to use cost estimates that worked in every part of the country. It was 2011 or 2012, and iPads and cloud computing were new technologies. Meanwhile, you've got a forty- or fifty-year-old blue-collar worker who's used to swinging hammers—maybe a foreman running a crew.

"We launched this slick cloud computing software that, at the time, was going over 3G networks, so it was slow and clunky," Joe continues. "All these dudes had $600 iPads to use with our cloud computing technology, but what they used them for instead was as a hard surface to put their yellow pad on so they could take all their notes! Then they would take their yellow pads home and use their big, clunky PCs to figure out the job costs. It was constant stuff like that. But as regional director, I watched a lot of the growth, all the way from buying our first house."

## Bernanke Sinks Us

However, with the excitement of expansion came that relentless background drumbeat: *raise capital, raise capital, raise capital.* If we were to keep going, we had to do that on an unprecedented level—raise a half a billion dollars at least—and we had to get it from the public markets. We had started building an IPO-quality executive team in 2012, and now we resumed that effort.

The timing seemed perfect. By early 2013, when we started making serious public offering plans, the institutional investor world had become used to the idea of REITs as public corporations. In December 2012, Silver Bay, a small SFR REIT, became the first single-family REIT to go public, raising $245 million with its stock offering. It was like someone flipped a switch. Investors suddenly said, "Oh, we can invest in single-family rental through the public markets now?" Demand exploded. Other companies started gearing up to go public.

Around the same time, interest in the large private equity deals that had been our lifeblood dried up. Private equity investors typically demand 20 percent returns, and we had no way of underwriting that. Underwriting on our early deals had shown a 20 percent internal rate of return, and we had hit that number. But that was in 2009 and 2010, when housing prices were much lower and there was tremendous appreciation "baked into" the Bay Area real estate market.

By 2013, homes had already appreciated so much that a 20 percent return was unrealistic. It was also difficult for us to create a reliable model on houses that we still hadn't purchased. Public market investors, on the other hand, are willing to take lower returns because they have greater liquidity. They can sell their stock and cash out whenever they like. Public markets became our best option for securing capital in amounts that could be game changing.

Our plan was to go public on our own. We had phenomenal growth numbers, a proven business model, a top-notch executive team, and a market environment where our business was suddenly sexy. Then, on June 19, 2013, fed chairman Ben Bernanke gave a speech in which he said that the Federal Reserve was likely to curtail the bond purchases known as quantitative easing—basically, buying government bonds to increase the money supply. *Boom.* His words were like dropping a nuclear bomb on the REIT market. Interest rates jumped, and the FTSE Nareit All REITs Index—an index that tracks the value of all public real estate investment trusts—dropped by 10 percent.

Companies talk about the "window closing" on their IPO, and our window had just slammed shut on our fingers. People who had been salivating over the prospect of investing in SFR through the public markets got nervous and ran in the other direction. The appetite for IPOs in the space dropped to nothing. A few days later, another REIT IPO was canceled. Reluctantly, we got the message: *we cannot go public right now.*

While all this was going on, the inevitable had happened: the SFR market had become ferociously competitive. Multibillion-dollar private equity companies like Blackstone, Invitation, and Starwood had finally become aware of the dynamics in the single-family market, done their due diligence, and decided there were profits to be made. They didn't know the market as well as we did, but they had long-standing banking relationships and bottomless wells of capital, and big money can cover up for a lot of big mistakes. As big as Waypoint had become, we were a minnow compared to some of the sharks swimming in what had been our calm part of the ocean.

Our leading position in the sailboat race had bought us a little time, but our need for capital had not changed. We had burned through our most recent round of private funds as well as our Citibank loan, and we were once again in the familiar position of needing capital and having perhaps two months of cash left to run Waypoint. We were in trouble, and we were *tired* of being in trouble. Going public would solve our endless capital issues, so we went back to that idea. But now, thanks to chairman Bernanke's words, SFR investors had developed a nervous twitch about IPOs in the REIT sector. Waypoint was too small to go public alone. If we wanted to tap public markets, we would need to merge with another company.

## Finding Starwood Capital

We started talking with every private equity investor that had dabbled in the SFR space, attempting to figure out if there was a potential partnership to be had. Our perfect scenario was a private equity investor with lots of capital and a desire to be in the space but without a management team or an operating platform that would get in our way. We knew how to make SFR profitable. We had the management team and the operating platform; we just needed access to capital. In the summer of 2013, we met with everyone and anyone who fit our profile.

We wound up dancing with a changing roster of partners. First, we tried to figure out who was interested. Next, we determined which company would be the best fit for us. Finally, we laid out what we thought a good deal with that company looked like. There was interest: for a while, we were negotiating with three groups concurrently, playing them off each other, pushing hard for a favorable deal. It was kind of funny. Players with a lot of capital were accustomed to everyone rolling over for them and giving them what they want, so we surprised them by being tough negotiators and saying "No" often. Unfortunately, we negotiated so hard that everyone said, "You know what? This isn't for us."

Everyone except for Starwood Capital.

Remember when we told you that big news has always seemed to happen when one or both of us was on summer vacation? True to form, Doug was with his family at Lake Tahoe when negotiations with Starwood got real. He had to leave his family in the middle of their trip to sit down with Barry Sternlicht. Barry is cofounder, chairman, and CEO of Starwood Capital Group, which today has more than $50 billion in assets under management, and chairman of Starwood Property Trust, the largest commercial mortgage REIT in the country. Barry is a player—brilliant, intense, and a tough negotiator.

Barry wanted to have lunch with us the next day in New York, so we got on a plane. At lunch, we discussed what a merger between Starwood and Waypoint might look like and what the terms might be. We also surprised Barry when we revealed that after the 2013 article had come out and we knew the FBI investigation was over, we had agreed to resume our positions as corporate officers. Doug and Gary Beasley would serve as co-CEOs, while Colin would be Waypoint's chief investment officer. Taken aback, Barry said, "You guys were half retired and now you want to be in the company, and you want co-CEOs? That's the stupidest thing I ever heard. Why would you ever have a co-CEO?"

Despite that and a few other bumps, on November 1, 2013, it was announced that Starwood Property Trust would spin off its single-family residential business into a new REIT with a portfolio of more than eight thousand single-family homes: Starwood Waypoint Residential Trust—SWAY, for short. Our goal was to begin trading under that ticker symbol on the New York Stock Exchange as a public company as early as February 2014.

We weren't going to go public on our own, but we were going to do it. We had sailed our boat to a big lead and built something that would trade on the NYSE. It was a big moment.

## Dog and Pony Show

However, even though SWAY was technically a spin-off of two well-established companies, we still had to do the usual pre-IPO roadshow. That's where the principals in a company that's about to go public travel to all the centers of financial power to deliver the same spiel about their business until their brains begin to hemorrhage.

That's an exaggeration, but not by much. Gary and Doug were the point men for the SWAY road show, and it was our job to convince big institutional investors—banks, insurance companies, mutual funds, pensions, hedge funds, endowments—that buying our stock would be the smartest move they ever made. So three weeks before we were scheduled to go public we headed off on a trip to the financial centers of the Northeast: Boston, Philadelphia, Baltimore, New York. We would fly on a private jet for maximum speed and flexibility.

You know that saying about the best-laid plans of mice and men going awry? Well, everything we touched on our road show went awry. All we could do was laugh about it, and we did. As we left on the trip, a huge blizzard buried the Northeast. All airports were shut down, which meant our private jet was grounded. We scrambled and got seats on the train from Boston to New York, but it wasn't the speedy Acela train. No, we ended up on the local, so we got to make stops in New England towns like Brookline, Canton, Mansfield, and Attleboro—until the train broke down.

It's funny now, but then it was beyond frustrating: The entire Starwood Waypoint brain trust stuck on the tracks in the middle of nowhere, sending pictures of us drinking beers from the cafeteria cart to our team back home. It ended up taking us about seven hours to get to Manhattan, by which time all we could do was laugh. We were so punchy that everything was funny.

Here's the other thing about road shows: You might take forty or fifty meetings when you're on one, but for all intents and purposes they will be exactly the same meeting. They practically follow a checklist:

- **Step One:** Walk into a conference room that's superficially different from the last one you were in but still contains a long wooden table, glasses and pitchers of water, a speakerphone, and a whiteboard, just like every other room.
- **Step Two:** Take a seat opposite men and women who all went to Wharton, Stanford, MIT, and Columbia and who, despite their polite smiles, look at you like you're a door-to-door salesman who's making them late for their afternoon squash game.
- **Step Three:** Deliver the same speech about your company you just gave to the last group and present your financial data.
- **Step Four:** Respond to questions so predictable that you could do Johnny Carson's old Carnac the Magnificent routine and answer them before they're asked.
- **Step Five:** Shake hands, say thank you, and stagger to the next office.
- **Step Six:** Repeat.

You might do that ten times in a single day. It becomes mind numbing. Plus, each meeting might take forty-five minutes, leaving us fifteen minutes to race to our next meeting. Nina Tran, the CFO who saved our sanity when nobody could make any sense of our books, was with us in New York in the middle of that blizzard, and she wound up walking from one meeting to the next in the deep, slushy Manhattan snow, in heels, dragging her suitcase behind her.

"You're meeting ten or eleven different investors in a day," she says. "So you go from one meeting to another. When we were on the East Coast, a lot of times we ran late for a meeting, and instead of hopping into our transportation to go to the next meeting, because there was so much traffic in Manhattan, we would walk from one location to another to get there on time. The guys were in their dress shoes, but I'm in heels. And I'm the only woman.

"During one road show in New York and Boston, we had to come home for an all-hands meeting. By the time we got back to New York, there were two feet of snow that we didn't expect. Let's just say I didn't have the right footwear at all. At the end of the day, it was me trying to keep up in my heels with all these guys marching to the next meeting. It was a bit crazy and quite tiring. But at the same time, you look back and you laugh. Because we did have fun, even though it was monotonous."

After a few days, we became so desperate to break the monotony that we started making inside jokes. One was to take expressions that meant something to us but no one else and work them into our presentations. We started giving each other points for weaving this or that phrase into our talking points. For example, when someone asked about the time it had taken to build Waypoint, one of our standard rebuttals was that no matter how many people you have, it takes time to build a technology platform that adds value to an industry. Our go-to phrase about this became, "A woman can have a baby in nine months, but nine women can't have a baby in one month."

Gary Beasley was there, and he remembers how ridiculous and pants-wettingly funny the whole thing got. "One of the funniest things was that Colin always had a problem getting that baby line straight," he says. "Colin would try to work it into the talk and start it off by saying, 'Nine babies—wait a second.' Everyone would be looking at him like, 'What are you talking about?' One of us would try to jump in and save it." When our hosts furrowed their brows at that gibberish, it took every ounce of self-control we had to keep from doubling over with helpless laughter.

Before long, it was all any of us could do to keep a straight face when Colin repeated, "A woman can have a baby in nine months, but nine women can't have a baby in one month" for the sixth or seventh time and saw the heads on the other side of the table nodding as though we'd said something profound. We weren't being rude. We were punch-drunk.

Another time, Colin said, "Waypoint is the Apple of single-family rentals," whatever the hell that meant. Were we saying we were innovative? That we had a terrific user experience? That we were a cult? We had no idea, but it sounded good. There were times we barely made it to the elevator before breaking up like a pack of hyenas because we had all tried working that line into our spiel.

By the end of the road show, we were delirious. We were simply trying not to fall apart laughing *during* meetings. We continued trying to set each other off while we were sitting across from potential investors. On one occasion, Gary was with us, and we were rattling off the usual lines about SWAY. We looked down, and we were all gripping our legs, white knuckled, trying to keep ourselves from breaking into hysterical laughter.

In our last meeting with PIMCO, the big investment manager, our discipline cracked. Several times during the meeting, we broke into laughter. When we left, our faces hurt and we were practically crying. In the elevator, we said, "They're not going to give us a dime." Then we got to the really important part: comparing who had worked more of our go-to clichés into the meeting and giving each other points—two for Colin, one for Gary, and so on. It was just something to do, but it helped us survive the road show without losing what was left of our marbles. And as it turned out, our efforts were very successful. Investors understood what we were doing and loved our business model.

## February 3, 2014

Starwood Waypoint Residential Trust went public on February 3, 2014. This was the culmination of our determination to go long on an opportunity no one else had seen. It was the result of six years of being told it couldn't be done, then trying to find the money to get it done, then fending off the FBI and huge competitors who wanted to derail what we had gotten done. But we had done it.

Technically, we had not made an initial public offering, which is when you sell new shares to the market. Instead, we had spun shares out of Starwood's Mortgage REIT into a new REIT dedicated to single-family rentals. But the effect was the same. We had seen what others could not, taken on tremendous risk, worked harder than ever before, and built something that changed the real estate market.

We were all invited to ring the NYSE opening bell on the first day that SWAY traded publicly. We had the whole management team on the podium, our wives and kids on the floor of the NYSE watching, and everyone was very excited. This was a *big* deal, like getting to the top of Everest. This was the culmination of six years of hard work and sacrifice. It was an unforgettable event for everyone, from our families to our colleagues. It also boiled down everything we had worked for to a tangible moment in time, like saying, "You finally made it."

The thing is, when you're up there, it's not that intuitive. People think there's this big red button and that's it, but there are several buttons. So we were actually a little nervous. We didn't want to hit the wrong button and crash the stock market or something. On top of that, there's something about us, Manhattan, and a blizzard, because the day we were supposed to ring the bell there was a massive snowstorm.

On top of all that, everyone in Doug's family had been passing around a gastrointestinal bug for about a week. By the time the day came to ring the bell, Doug was the sickest he'd ever been in his life and had been vomiting all night and morning. Our trip to the NYSE hadn't been a fifteen-minute meet and greet; it had been a celebratory breakfast and a tour, and all through it poor Doug was running to the bathroom and puking. At breakfast, they asked Gary and us to stand up and say a few words, and Doug could barely stand up.

At the bell-ringing ceremony, he carried a barf bag with him to the podium and had mapped out a path to the nearest restroom in his head so he could sprint there, just in case. Despite all that, we rang the bell, our team had its moment in the sun, SWAY went public, and everyone was delighted. The cycle of endless fundraising was over. Our company was secure. Everything from this point on would be perfect.

# CHAPTER SEVEN

# Bigger Isn't Always Better

You don't have to go long on your idea. You can choose to keep your idea relatively small and under your control and still build a very successful company. We know many entrepreneurs who've made exactly that choice. However, it depends on your goals. If your goal is to build something that can transform an entire industry, you've got to go big. When you do, you should know that the business you thought you had under your tight control can quickly accelerate out of your control, until you're like a terrified joyride passenger holding on for dear life.

We knew that if we were ever going to escape the endless cycle of raising capital and be able to run the business we had built, we had to take Waypoint public. There was simply no other option left open to us. But we also knew there was every chance that the act of taking our company public would turn it into a business that we didn't want to run anymore. To paraphrase Morpheus from *The Matrix*, the market, it seems, is not without a sense of irony.

Don't get us wrong. Taking a company public is every entrepreneur's dream, and we had managed to build something that people wanted to invest in. We were proud of our achievement. But even before we agreed to follow the public path and seek an M&A partner, we knew that the cost of keeping our company growing might be walking away from it. In the early days, when we started to think that Waypoint had the potential to become a public company sometime in the future, we made a handshake deal. Colin made it clear that if we ever went public, he probably would not want to stay. Of course, the odds of any company, especially a young one like ours, going public were so remote that we promptly forgot about the agreement.

And yet, there we were.

What's so bad about running a public company, and why would an entrepreneur who had worked incredibly hard to build one want to walk away from it? You can see part of the answers in interviews on the subject with heavyweights like Elon Musk and Michael Dell. They talk candidly about the unpleasant side of running a public corporation: stifling regulation, quarterly earnings reports, conference calls with the financial press, constant scrutiny, not being able to take risks, and having to change your business model to satisfy Wall Street's appetite for constant growth, to name a few—plus, the specter of losing control of what you built from nothing, which happens to founders quite frequently.

It all boils down to this: when you go public, you don't get to be an entrepreneur anymore. The only thing entrepreneurs and executives have in common is that both words start with *e*. Entrepreneurs can go big and take crazy risks. They can dare to dream about disrupting entire industries, be creative, and treat failure as one more stepping-stone on the path to success. Running a public corporation demands conservatism. Risk and creativity are constrained by the need to be predictable and meet expectations and by the hunger for constant revenue growth. The environments could not be more different, and we both knew it.

## Growing Pains

After SWAY went public, we created the role of chief investment officer for Colin, but he was true to his word. One year and two months after we went public, in April 2015, he left Starwood Waypoint. Co-CEO Gary Beasley also left around the same time, and suddenly Doug was the last man standing. Imagine, after working together for years and standing side by side in the glaring spotlight of a public offering, in the space of a few months, your entire support system is gone. It was disorienting.

Colin was living the good life, which included hanging out with the likes of Richard Branson and TED founder Chris Anderson. He was also reading a book called *Exponential Organizations* by Salim Ismail, the founding executive director of Singularity University, which offers a great perspective on how exponential technologies—microprocessor speed doubling per Moore's law, network bandwidth doubling, the ubiquity of mobile devices, artificial intelligence, the drop in the cost of memory—are transforming industries and creating new ones. Later on, those ideas will become very relevant to our story.

Back in 2015, Doug was trying to hold down the fort at Starwood Waypoint, but all was not well. Doug really likes to manage people; he was one of the big reasons Waypoint had such a tight-knit culture. But the new public company was much larger and more complex, making hands-on personnel management impossible. That's okay; it's important to be able to adapt to changing circumstances, and when you do, you grow. However, Doug was able to do little of what he had enjoyed at Waypoint. He spent about one-third of his time preparing to talk about quarterly earnings or answering questions from investors about earnings. The other two-thirds went to running the company. The people part got left behind.

## Mergers and Acquisitions

Also, the SFR industry was beginning to consolidate, putting more pressure on Starwood Waypoint to continue growing. By 2015, it was clear that single-family REITs would perform better at scale. This eventually set off a lot of merger and acquisition activity in the space. For example, in 2015, Silver Bay Realty Trust, the first REIT to go public, acquired more than two thousand rental homes from the American Home, while in March 2016, single-family rental giants American Homes 4 Rent and American Residential Properties, Inc. completed their merger.

Meanwhile, SWAY was having its challenges. The company needed to grow, but the stock price was below book value, which meant that we couldn't raise new equity. We had gone public to raise money, but we never expected our stock price to be so low that we couldn't actually raise it. It was a real conundrum, and it led us to look at an alternative path to growth: another merger.

Things finally came to a head in the summer of 2015. Doug

was in Bergen, Norway, on vacation with his family, and yes, the infamous "vacation curse" struck again. The Briens were traveling into a fjord, and when they finally got to a town that had cell reception, Doug found that he had multiple messages from Brendan Brogen, the senior VP of acquisitions at Starwood Waypoint. Doug returned the call and learned that Barry was talking to Tom Barrack at Colony Capital about merging with his company, Colony American Homes. Standing there with the phone in his hand, Doug wondered if this was the right move for the company—and how much say he would have in the deal.

This brings up another big downside of going public if you're an entrepreneur: You don't get to make the calls anymore. Your board does. In a hasty midnight conference call with the board, Doug learned that Tom Barrick, who runs Colony Capital, had made Barry an offer he couldn't refuse. Barry controlled the company, so the deal was going to happen.

Doug's role? To be determined. However, even though he didn't love the way it went down, it was clear that the merger was the right move for SWAY.

## Colony American Homes

The plan was to announce this complex merger—which would create a new company, Colony Starwood Homes, with about thirty-five thousand homes and a combined asset value of $7.7 billion—in January 2016. But first, the team had to figure out how to put this new company together in six months, including choosing a CEO. All our friends who had been through big mergers said that the CEO from the larger company usually took the big chair in the new entity. But with his background in day-to-day operations, we felt Doug was the right person to run the show.

He met with Tom and Barry to pitch them on why he was the man to steer the new Colony Starwood Homes. Barry and Doug had become friends and had a great deal of respect for each other. Barry believed in Doug and wanted him to be the CEO. However, he told Doug that "we" ultimately had to sell Tom Barrick because he controlled the controlling company in this merger.

"It was surreal," Doug says. "Tom invited me for breakfast at his mansion on a cliff overlooking the ocean in Santa Monica. It was just Tom, me, and our COO, Charles Young, and Charles and I were explaining why we could lead this company. We talked about our background, how we had built Waypoint from nothing, and how we would run the merged company. I learned later that we were wasting our time. Tom had already decided to name Colony copresident and COO Fred Tuomi, who had eighteen years of public market experience."

Doug wanted the job but recognized the logic of the decision. Fred would stabilize the merged company and develop credibility with the markets, and Doug would be the president and COO. But despite the promise of succeeding Fred as CEO "in a few years," Doug knew what this really was. It was a *demotion*. He had negotiated a healthy severance package before the Starwood merger, so walking away was tempting. But he would be walking away from the chance to ultimately be the CEO of a multi-billion-dollar public REIT. That was an opportunity that might never come again, even if it did come under less-than-ideal circumstances.

Doug decided that he couldn't pass up the challenge. However, he told Fred that if he stayed, he didn't want anyone looking over his shoulder or second-guessing his decisions. Fred agreed. So three months before the merger, it was officially announced that Fred would be CEO, while Doug would be president and COO. Everybody would live happily ever after.

## An Exponential Opportunity

In the weeks following, Doug and Colin were on the phone constantly. Doug was second-guessing his decision to stay. Had he made the right call? It was around that time that we started talking about the enormous, untapped market for rental property management services.

Remember that book we mentioned earlier, *Exponential Organizations*? One of its key points is that technology has the power to disrupt and transform untapped markets where technology hasn't been applied yet. One of those markets is the management of residential rental properties in the United States. According to US census data, the country has about twenty-three million single-family rentals with one to four units. If you expand that to include small multifamily buildings too small to have full-time employees with up to forty-nine units, you get an industry twice as big as the hotel industry. Managing those properties is a $29 billion business that almost no one knows about.

Part of the reason nobody knows about it is because it's very fragmented. Only 35 to 40 percent of rental owners use a third-party management company, and a lot of those companies are local mom-and-pop shops with just a few employees. The rest of the owners self-manage. Around the time we started talking about the industry in 2016, the largest company in the rental management space had a microscopic market share of only 0.14 percent. This was a pie with a lot of room to grow.

Just as the emergence of cloud computing and powerful mobile devices had helped us build the platform that made Waypoint possible, technology now makes it possible for innovative entrepreneurs to identify hidden value in a business sector, develop a technology platform that can exploit that value, and turn a sleepy or even nonexistent industry into an economic powerhouse.

For instance, when smart, tech-enabled companies like Uber and Lyft entered the transportation space, they didn't just take away a share of the pie from taxi companies. They grew the pie. Instead of offering the same product as medallion taxi services, shippers like UPS, or delivery brands like DoorDash, they found untapped value in the giant fleet of private vehicles that spent most of their time sitting in people's driveways. By using technologies like wireless data, GPS, and artificial intelligence, they built platforms that created an industry from nothing: independent drivers using their own vehicles to deliver people and parcels to destinations. Talk about disruption!

We saw that same potential in the world of rental management. It was already a massive industry that no one was doing at scale, where billions in potential revenue were being left on the table because nobody had a way to deliver greater speed, efficiency, and renter service. And we thought we might be able to do it. Very quickly, we saw that the residential rental sector was an opportunity that might dwarf Waypoint.

## Property Management 101

To understand why the opportunity was so extraordinary, you have to understand what property management is. It's really just a bunch of decisions people have to make and implement about five core functions:

1. Leasing vacant units
2. Managing repairs and maintenance and turning over units for new residents
3. Collecting rent
4. Communicating with owners and residents
5. Reporting

For as long as there have been rental properties and people to rent them, these five concerns have been handled the same way. A landlord has a vacant unit, so his management company places an ad. Potential renters call, make appointments to see the property, and provide information for a credit check. Based largely on gut instinct, the landlord chooses the renter least likely to skip out on the rent or grow marijuana in the bathroom. The renter signs a paper contract, and they get the keys.

If repairs and maintenance are needed, it's usually up to the renter to call the management office and leave a message. Eventually, a property manager or superintendent comes over to inspect the problem and determine what to do next. Let's say there's no hot water. If the manager agrees the water heater is dead, he calls around to find a contractor who can pick up a new unit and come over to install it. This might take a week, during which time the renter has no hot water. Meanwhile, routine maintenance—cleaning gutters, checking the roof, changing HVAC filters, and a hundred other tasks—gets overlooked because management spends all its time putting out repair fires.

Collecting rent runs smoother because even some old-guard

property managers use electronic payment platforms now. However, if they don't, landlords have to wait for renters to mail or drop off paper checks, which can put a serious crimp in cash flow. Communication and reporting are analog, done via the US Postal Service, if they're done at all.

There are dozens of points in this antiquated system where the right technology can add value. For example, decisions about renters, rents, contractors, and more can be automated using artificial intelligence and predictive analytics, using data on past activity patterns to drive decisions in real time.

After all, what are people doing when they manage rentals? They're making decisions about repairs, scheduling, who will be an ideal renter, and so on. They're communicating with owners, residents, and vendors. Technology can make those communications seamless. If you order lunch from DoorDash, you don't wait on hold or speak with anyone. You make a decision, and that decision is conveyed to the service provider. Unless there's a problem and humans need to step in, communication is automated. You get a text confirming your order, a text letting you know when your order is on the way, and one more informing you that your delivery person has arrived. Why not incorporate that efficiency into residential rental management?

You could argue that there's a sixth function in property management—managing renter needs and complaints—but we disagree. If you do the other five well, you eliminate a lot of headaches. Use data and predictive analytics to select well-behaved, responsible renters, and you minimize complaints. Keep up on maintenance and handle repairs with high efficiency, and you keep renters happy while preventing system failures and mechanical breakdowns.

## The Frictionless Rental Experience

The twenty-first century will be about white-collar jobs being automated—*thinking* being more automated—rather than physically moving things. In property management, this paradigm shift is not about eliminating people, because people are still great at problem-solving. Instead, it's about eliminating unnecessary communication so that people can use their time and resources to make better decisions and develop better solutions.

For example, predictive analytics can put all the information about maintenance tasks for five hundred rentals in front of a property manager so they can schedule and assign tasks much faster and more easily than picking up a phone and calling vendors one at a time. No more hoping that Joe the tile guy is available to fix the leaking shower pan in one of your properties. Now you can look at a dashboard on your iPhone and see in real time who's busy and who's available for an emergency job.

At Waypoint, we'd had our eye on the property management industry for years. It was begging to be disrupted and technologized. In fact, we did some of that at Waypoint. For example, in leasing, instead of having someone meet a prospective renter at a property, we did self-showings. Each house had a smart lock, and we could text someone a temporary code they could use to get into the house. They would tour the house on their own and decide if they wanted to rent it or not. Because all entries were time-coded, we knew exactly who was in each property when, in case there was theft or vandalism (which there never was). By giving people quick access instead of making them wait to meet with a rental agent, we found we could get more leases signed faster.

We've really refined this today. Today, if a resident comes to our website from Zillow or Craigslist, they can click on a listing to schedule a self-showing. They get their code via text, walk through the unit, and while they're in the unit, they receive a text message inviting them to apply to rent it. If they like the unit, they can fill out an application right there on their phone (while they're standing in the unit) or on a computer later. We screen them through our credit agency algorithm, and if we approve them, they can submit a security deposit on the spot using their banking app. Later, we'll send them an electronic lease to sign, and then they can schedule their move-in. Renters love this system because it's fast and efficient, and there's no rental agent following them from room to room, tapping her foot impatiently.

At Waypoint, we also had a method for using data to rate our leasing prospects. Previously, we'd reviewed the hundreds of leasing inquiries coming in daily one at a time—an incredible waste of time. Then we developed a machine-learning algorithm that optimized inquiries based on how likely a person was to rent the unit based on a number of factors—including, surprisingly, the time of day they applied. For some reason, people who inquire during business hours are more likely to lease a place than people who inquire early in the morning or in the evenings. We found strong correlations in the data that told us who was more likely to sign a lease, and we prioritized those people.

Before the Colony merger, Doug had approached the Starwood Waypoint leadership team about going into the property management business. His pitch was simple: the single-family rental market was becoming overcrowded, and the competition for rental homes was becoming fierce. Meanwhile, there was a giant, overlooked mom-and-pop segment of the economy that was ripe for disruption using technology . . . and no one was acting on the opportunity. He made a convincing argument that SWAY could add third-party property management to its business model and be the first to leverage this huge market.

The board was uninterested. They felt that a rental management play was not in line with what the investors or shareholders wanted. That is part of the reality of being a public company with certain fiduciary obligations, but it's also an excellent illustration of our point at the beginning of the chapter—a maddening example of how public companies kill entrepreneurial thinking. While a hungry, agile young company might have jumped at the chance to get into the rental management market, a public corporation simply would not take that kind of risk.

## The Seventy-Five-Dollar Bottle of Wine that Broke the Camel's Back

With the Colony merger just around the corner and SWAY uninterested in exploring the rental management market, Doug was restless and frustrated in his job as president and COO. Worst of all, rather than honor his no-interference pledge, Fred was doing the opposite. The final straw came when Doug took everybody on his new team out to a nice get-to-know-you dinner. The goal was to break bread, talk, and start building some trust, but then he got pushback from Fred for spending seventy-five dollars on a bottle of wine. This soon-to-be $7 billion corporation called out its COO over a nice bottle of Chardonnay.

That was, effectively, the end. In his mind, Doug was gone, even though he wouldn't physically leave for some time. He said later, "I didn't want a job, and I wanted the freedom to do things the way I wanted." This is where knowing who you are pays dividends. Doug is a creative-minded team and company builder, so he tried to work within the soon-to-be merged company, but he found that he couldn't. It was against his nature. We are both entrepreneurs. We love taking risks and building things. Life is too short to do work that doesn't make you happy, and this role wasn't making him happy.

It was late 2015, and Starwood Waypoint and Colony were close to their official merger date. Fred had made a big public announcement about it. Doug knew that his departure would cause trouble for the two companies at this sensitive time, and he regretted that. Despite their disagreements, he thought Fred was a terrific guy and a knowledgeable executive and still thinks highly of him to this day. They ended up parting on great terms. But the situation was not right for him, and if he couldn't give the job his all, he had an obligation to leave.

Finally, Doug met with Barry and said, "This isn't working." Barry wanted him to stay because he felt Doug was teed up to be the next CEO and would be great at the job. However, he heard Doug out and ultimately agreed with him. The company would have to file a Form 8-K, a report to the SEC of unscheduled material events or corporate changes at the company that could be important to shareholders. They did that and had Doug make the announcement at an earnings call.

On January 1, 2016, a few days before the official press release announcing the merger, Doug officially left. He took a nice severance package, and he had planned on taking a few months off to destress and maybe take an uninterrupted vacation. But that's not how it worked out. By May 2016, we launched our new rental management company, Mynd.

# CHAPTER EIGHT

# Go Long, Round Two

We already knew that managing single-family rentals was a mostly low-tech $29 billion business where the largest franchise player had just one-seventh of 1 percent of the market. Take out the 70 percent of SFR owners who managed their own properties, and you were left with a service provider class that you're probably familiar with if you ever rented an apartment after college: the hometown property management office.

Everyone can readily call up a mental picture of what one of these operations is like. You have a husband and wife overseeing a handful of employees, a website designed in 2008, and a dingy office in a local strip mall. The wife answers the phones, runs credit checks, and sends out lease agreements via snail mail; the husband handles the service calls and does most of the maintenance himself. The operation is slow to respond to tenant concerns and has no tech backbone whatsoever—maybe an aol.com email address.

Our experience building a rental management system at Waypoint had convinced us that tech-enabled rental management could offer both renters and landlords greater efficiency and more cost savings, while delivering a superior experience for everyone. By the time Doug left Colony Starwood Waypoint Homes in 2016, we both knew that same concept could be the basis for a terrific stand-alone company. It was time to bring that business into being—to go long for a second time.

Mynd's business model takes the disorganized activities of rental management and uses technology to make them more easily manageable. We use analytics to sift through data on potential renters and identify the ones with the highest probability of paying their rent on time and taking care of the properties. That enables Mynd to make better decisions. Full-stack platforms like ours create value by providing a single central access point where services can be ordered, communications carried out, and transactions securely completed, all in seconds with a few taps on a screen.

Because we were building a platform, we didn't have to own the assets with Mynd like we did with Waypoint. Our technology would simply enable economic activity and let all parties get more value out of their activities. It's the same model you see with Netflix and Uber, among others. Uber doesn't own its cars, and despite investing about $14 billion in original content, Netflix doesn't own most of the movies it streams. Not owning assets took away the constant pressure to raise capital, which let us focus on building a sensational company.

## Making Things Better

We already had everything we needed to build Mynd. Our experience building Waypoint from the ground up had given us a post-grad-level education in the software, hardware, datasets, and processes we would need, and we knew SFR backward and forwards.

At Waypoint, when we bought another house, we could add it into our property management system like adding another node on a network. It was easy. So we said, "What if we institutionalized the property management industry? What if we created a property management platform that landlords and property managers could access from their smartphones?" As with the early days of Waypoint, to the best of our knowledge, there was nobody else in the space. This was another once-in-a-lifetime opportunity that we couldn't walk away from.

We didn't create Mynd to kill off the low-tech, mom-and-pop property management business. We simply wanted to build an alternative so the owners of one or two rental properties—not to mention the owners of large SFR portfolios—could have access to the same tools we built for the Wall Street pros at Waypoint. We also knew that because of technology, business was changing. Mom-and-pop industries that have run the same way for decades were being challenged. Of course, we'd still have bodegas and beauty salons, local retail stores and restaurants. But technology is a terrific tool for revealing hidden value in parts of the economy and enabling entrepreneurs to create efficiencies to leverage that value. That's what we hoped to do. We didn't see it as writing the obituary for the mom-and-pop business, and we still don't.

Instead, our goal was to make things better for everyone in the rental ecosystem—to be part of the solution. That's always been our business compass. People tend to think of technology and innovation as negative forces. They destroy jobs, displace people, reduce customer choice for the sake of enriching a few shareholders . . . you know the narrative. And yes, that does happen. But it doesn't have to be that way. Business doesn't have to be predatory. You can solve problems, create prosperity, be sustainable, *and* make a profit all at the same time. That's what we've always aspired to.

The 2008 housing collapse was a crisis with a human face. Families were losing their homes, and homes are tied to where the kids go to school. Once these houses were abandoned and became dilapidated, neighborhoods and then communities started to die. When we started Waypoint, we didn't want to profit off of that kind of human toll. We wanted to help fix it.

We said, "What if we don't just rent out houses? What if we thoughtfully create a business model that appeases our investors and attracts the right renters—renters who want to be owners? We could serve everybody." We both loved the idea. Being part of the solution, rather than simply profiting off the problem, was in Waypoint's DNA from the start.

That separated us from the hedge fund investors who were the subject of *The Big Short*. Their goal was to make incredible profits off the collapse of the financial system. We find it easier to do business when you're the "good guys." That helped us attract and keep great employees and earn the trust of our investors. Back when we were under FBI investigation and in the middle of trying to raise capital and we told our bankers about being subpoenaed, they shrugged it off. They did that because they knew we were good guys who were trying to do things the right way. It matters.

## Another Day, Another Disruption

With Mynd, we would apply the technology that powered Waypoint to open up new efficiency and value in the rental management space for individual investors. Our platform would make things faster, more transparent, more frictionless, and more profitable for property owners, property managers, and people in the building trade. We would transform an industry that was overdue for transformation.

We also figured that our solution would unlock layers of value in the rental economy that we couldn't even anticipate. That's one of the hallmarks of tech highfliers that are really full-service platforms. Think about Uber again as an example. Whatever you might think about the company, not only has it created flexible employment for millions of people and forced legacy taxi companies to adapt, it has also spun off unanticipated value centers, hundreds of companies that service small slivers of the ride-hailing economy.

Mynd would be a robust, full-stack platform that would transform the rental management sector. We would include some of our greatest hits from Waypoint—self-showings, instant credit checks, lease signing on mobile devices—but we would build in a host of other features we knew property owners would love, including:

- **Automatic lease renewal**. When a resident's lease was close to expiring, they would receive multiple automated messages reminding them of the option to renew. It was literally as simple as "Your lease will expire on this date" with different rent options. The system would offer different rent amounts for different lease terms, with higher rents for the terms we didn't want, such as a contract that expired in December, when it's nearly impossible to rent a place. We would keep sending emails, and the renters would see the rent amounts changing, which was a subtle incentive to make a choice.

Any time before the expiration of their current lease, the resident could sign a new lease on their phone and be in the property for another year. No snail mail, no delays, no phone calls, and a higher rate of lease renewal than the old way. If a resident wasn't desirable, we could choose not to send them those reminders.

- **Data mining to predict tenant quality**. Landlords and investors pay attention to how long it takes to lease a property and how much the person pays in rent, but whom you rent to is actually the most important factor in profitability. You want people who will pay and stay, because that reduces turnover and improves cash flow. You want people who will take care of your assets, because people who don't care for the places they live in cost owners a fortune. (Remember the horrific postforeclosure vandalism we saw early on?) Right away, we realized that using big data and predictive analytics to pre-screen residents could be a critical value point.

A lot of landlords insist on sitting down with a prospective renter, thinking they can judge whether the person will be a good resident based on subjective factors. They'll say things like, "I want to look them in the eye." Well, fair housing laws make that illegal, and it also doesn't work. With Waypoint, we found that we could use all kinds of data to tell us if a person was likely to be a good tenant. After we had enough data, we'd go back once a quarter and ask, "What do the most successful residents do?" Answer: they stay, they pay, and they pass inspections.

We also defined bad residents: they pay late, they fail their inspections, and they don't take care of the property. We used data to create a box around the ideal resident, a collection of correlations that told us someone was likely to be a good renter. That way we could recognize those people in the future and do a better job of picking good residents. We had to study their attributes to figure that out.

What kind of correlations point the way to a good resident? Believe it or not, one piece of information that's shockingly prescient is your commute time from your job to your home. That data point is great at predicting how successful you will be at paying your rent or how long you will stay. People's social media profile and interactions are also surprisingly reflective of what they will be like as tenants. That's all public information, so it's legal to use it. When we were seeking funding for Mynd, this allowed us to go to venture capital firms and say, "We've created a better mousetrap for picking the best renters."

- **Setting precise rents**. With the shortage in affordable housing in many parts of the country, the rental market is much more competitive now. Setting rents has become a competition. It's not surprising that renters care about this: the 2018 Zillow Group Consumer Housing Trends Report found that 82 percent of renters find it extremely or very important that their home is within their budget.

However, there are all sorts of formulas and metrics that landlords are supposed to use to set rents. One is the "1 percent rule," which says that if you're renting a single-family home, the rent should be 1 percent of the home's market value. So if the home is worth $200,000, rent should be $2,000 a month. That seems logical, but it ignores many other factors, like local rents, local incomes, the kind of residents you want, and area rent control laws. At Mynd, we process a mountain of similar area rental data to tell landlords what their ideal rent should be on a property-by-property basis.

- **Vendor portal**. No more calling around to find a guy who's available to install crown molding or build a deck. Our vendor portal allows our renovation contractors and other approved vendors to log in, pull down jobs, and say, "I want to do that one." They're assigned the job automatically, and we already have their prices, licenses, and bonding. Our vendors don't even have to send us an invoice. When a job is done, an invoice is automatically generated, and they get paid right away, which they love.

  We also get better pricing from plumbers and other skilled vendors because we bring them a steady flow of good work and pay them right away. That's a great example of making things better for everyone—us, our residents, and our contractors.

- **Discounts.** At Waypoint, we were so large that we were one of Home Depot's five largest customers, so we were able to get a large discount. Now we're doing the same for all owners who contract with Mynd.

With those solutions and others in place, we were looking at an industry with nearly unlimited growth potential and a company that we were confident we could either take public one day or sell to a larger competitor. Waypoint had growth potential, but Mynd has much more. Waypoint's business model was based on owning and maintaining inventory, so we were dependent on the labor-intensive process of locating, underwriting, buying, and maintaining thousands upon thousands of properties. Not to mention we were fighting with well-funded competitors over a shrinking slice of pie. When we got to seventeen thousand homes, we hit a wall.

We took Waypoint as far as we could, but now, instead of buying and owning the real estate, we'd created a tech-enabled service platform that deals in bits, not molecules. Increasing capacity would be a matter of adding some server racks. However, our goal with Mynd was similar to our goal with Waypoint: *change the game.* With Waypoint, we helped to create a new asset class and got the investor markets to recognize its legitimacy. With Mynd, we were out to change the entire experience of owning and managing single-family rental properties.

We knew the market—a huge, low-tech, local industry that flew below the radar of the institutional investor community—and we knew its weaknesses. Mynd wouldn't be a solution provider selling tools to the incumbents. It would be a full-stack company *competing* with the incumbents, but doing it at scale with technology, creating efficiencies the legacy players couldn't match. We're creating a platform to extract optimal value from assets owned by other people. That's the business model that breeds exponential organizations like Uber and Airbnb. If we can make it all work, we'll change SFR for the second time. That's a chance no entrepreneur can pass up.

## Venture Capital

Another thing that's different about today is that in 2016, when we were ramping up Mynd, real estate technology was just beginning to take off. There were residential listing sites like Zillow and Trulia but nothing that compares to what's happening today. Real estate technology—proptech—has exploded in the last four years. It's one of the hottest sectors in venture capital.

However, this gold rush was still in the future when we were trying to raise Mynd's Series A. We had learned our lesson with Waypoint and had no interest in repeating the desperate, high-stress cycle of endlessly raising capital at the eleventh hour because we were running out of money. Plus, with Mynd, most of our capital wouldn't be going to buy assets that could be used as collateral, so debt was a smaller part of the equation. We needed to find third-party funding.

We self-funded our new company for a while, but then after three months, we went out to raise a Series A. It was a challenging pitch because the hype machine behind proptech hadn't started churning yet. Full-stack companies and end-to-end service platforms were nothing new, but they were relatively unproven in the real estate sector. We had some selling to do, and while we had raised money from individual investors and private equity firms, we had never raised it from venture capital firms.

*Venture capital.* The words bring up powerful images: huge, plush conference rooms, high-pressure pitches, and multimillion-dollar checks written to future unicorns. But while there's a little bit of truth to those stereotypes, the reality is that raising venture capital is selling, just like anything else. You're trying to build trust and credibility so that a group of powerful money managers will risk some of their investors' capital on you. That means coming to the table with a great idea and a bulletproof pitch but also having the poise and knowledge to answer tough questions, the patience to wait through what can be a long process, and the self-awareness to realize that just because you think your idea is brilliant doesn't mean everyone else will. You have to persuade them with your preparation, your understanding of the business you're in, and the uniqueness of your business model.

Our VC experience was great, but it had its challenges too. One of the tricky parts was that early on, we were preproduct and prerevenue. We had a company, a team, a track record, and a business plan that we knew was rock solid. Our data told us that. It also told us that the opportunity for the first mover in the market was *big*. But we were planning to build our own software from the ground up to do everything, and that's a heavy lift. That's expensive. Then we would launch the company, get customers, and grow.

We must have done something right, because in August 2016, we raised $5.5 million from Canaan Partners. That gave us the capital we needed to build the real estate industry's first property management mobile app—a very big deal in a fundraising and business climate where mobile functionality was *the* big thing. That helped us get to a Series A1 in 2017, where we raised another $5.1 million from Canaan, Jackson Square Ventures, Lightspeed Venture Partners, and some angel investors.

Raising that capital was incredibly freeing, because at Waypoint, we had been going out every six months, hat in hand, to raise capital from perhaps thirty investors. That meant endless meetings and phone calls, which took us away from operating the company. It was exhausting, like being on a financial hamster wheel. Now that was over. We had the cash to build Mynd.

But there was a downside too. With Waypoint, we were investing in tangible assets that everyone already knew had value. We didn't have to twist anybody's arm to make them see that owning Bay Area real estate at historic low prices was a good thing. With Mynd, the market didn't exist yet, at least not in the way we were envisioning it. While we were confident that SFR owners would embrace our platform after we showed them how much time, money, and frustration it would save them, we had no guarantee that we would get traction. Mynd was a bet that we could create something out of nothing.

In 2018, we raised a Series B round of $20 million with the same group of investors, taking our valuation to about $117 million, three times as high as our Series A valuation. Our Series A investors enjoyed a 300 percent markup on their investment in two years.

## Gains and Losses

With the dust settled, Mynd was a well-funded company, and we were able to act like entrepreneurs again. In part, that meant saying, "We know what we think is best, and we're going to make the best decisions we can, and nobody's going to second-guess us." That's never an option when you go public because the company doesn't belong to you anymore, not really. It belongs to your shareholders and to your board of directors. With Mynd, we were able to limber up our long-dormant risk muscles, get creative, and make gutsy calls without someone looking over our shoulders.

This is the trade-off entrepreneurs rarely talk about, because when the topic turns to taking a company public, everybody becomes obsessed with market capitalization and cashing out their stock options for early retirement. But the reality is this:

**You can have scale, or you can have freedom.**
**It's rare to have both.**

That's why some people become serial entrepreneurs. A liquidity event at one company lets them move on and start something new from scratch. They can build that company up, sell again, and move on. It becomes addictive, assuming you enjoy working long hours and willing a business into existence out of thin air—in effect, building the boat while sailing it. We enjoy it very much.

But there are always trade-offs. It's extremely difficult to build a business that can scale to the point where an IPO becomes possible and at the same time have the freedom to act like an entrepreneur 100 percent of the time. As we discovered with Waypoint, going long and thinking big often means setting aside every other priority in the pursuit of growth, growth, and more growth.

If you want your company to stay small and agile, good for you. Just be aware of the trade-offs. Also, good for you if you decide to scale a business to unicorn levels. With Waypoint, we knew we could build something big that would change the industry, and we were all in on that strategy. But there was a cost. Being a public corporation meant we could do less of what we love to do, which is to find untapped opportunities, get creative, and be entrepreneurs. We knew that going in, and when SWAY turned out not to be what we wanted, we left—each in our own time.

Life at Mynd hasn't been perfect, of course. At Waypoint, we owned the real estate, so we set rents and controlled repair and maintenance. Now we have hundreds of clients, landlords whose property management is affected by the decisions we make. We can't run every little decision by them, or we would never get anything done, but we're obligated to communicate and collaborate with our clients more than we did in the past. But we have a much, much simpler decision tree than we did as a public company, and that is a pleasure.

With Mynd, we have also enjoyed a different status in the start-up and business community than we did with Waypoint. We're a tech company, not a real estate company, and in the Bay Area and Silicon Valley, the difference is vast. Everybody wants to brand their company as a tech play (think about WeWork's Adam Neumann trying to brand coworking as a high-tech business because the company had a smartphone app) because in the minds of venture investors and shareholders, tech creates billionaires. We get interview requests from different press outlets than we did when we were at Waypoint, and the venture capital community sees us differently too. To this day, we receive regular invitations to join the advisory boards of other proptech companies because we know so much about the industry. It's flattering to be told that we add credibility and value just with our presence. It's a little like graduating to the big kids' table at Thanksgiving.

All of this is quite ironic, because while the value of technology can rise or fall in a month, real estate is a proven asset that *always* has value. Nevertheless, our technology platform made Mynd a hot property because it has the power to create efficiencies and scale effortlessly.

CHAPTER NINE

# Fundraise in a Pandemic and Learn a Lot

In the fall of 2019, we began working on our Series C funding round for Mynd. Our goal was to raise enough capital to power growth in a space that had become more and more competitive with every passing month. To meet our goal of lapping those competitors and capturing maximum market share, we needed more capital. We were pretty confident that if we started in October 2019, by early 2020, we would have a signed term sheet for the $60 million in new investment we were looking for.

If we had gone out earlier in 2019 with the numbers we had at the time, we would have been successful right away. We were considered a proptech company, and proptech was blowing up (in a good way) in early 2019. Then came the collapse of WeWork, and everything changed. Even though the rationale was flimsy, the capital markets had considered WeWork to be proptech, and when they were flying high and attracting $9 billion from SoftBank, the entire sector got a boost. When the perception of WeWork turned, everything changed.

The WeWork scandal cast a shadow over the entire industry. All of a sudden, growth equity investors worried that proptech was overvalued as a category, even though most of the start-ups were nothing like WeWork. When we went out to raise our round, we were suddenly faced with growing the company in a completely different paradigm. That's something we learned the hard way: if you as a start-up begin raising money in one capital paradigm and then the paradigm changes, you can find yourself running into a lot of friction. A lot of young companies fail when the capital paradigm changes.

Now we faced different questions and a lot more scrutiny. Before WeWork, everything was about, "How fast can you grow?" We were very focused on top-line revenue, which is what you do when investors perceive risk to be low and capital is plentiful. Then, virtually overnight, the questions were things like, "What's your burn rate? What are your gross margins? How long until you're profitable?"

Mynd was not set up for that. We had built a growth machine designed to capture market share and scale; profit would come later. In 2019, our board had told us that if we hit our numbers from 2018, we were going to kill it. Well, we hit our numbers, and we were *not* killing it. The ripple effect of WeWork ran through the public markets and the private capital markets and wrecked our ability to get financing. We were really on the ropes. We had the wrong track record and the wrong metrics for where the market was going.

Starting in the fall of 2019, we took meetings with more than one hundred potential investors. We walked away with one hundred and seventeen responses of "Thanks, but no thanks." *One hundred and seventeen rejections.* It was mind numbing. Remember, one of the hallmarks of the big long is that nobody will see what you see, and that's what was happening to us. It was hard to believe. Colin had been taking most of the meetings, but in January, he ran up the white flag. We realized that if Mynd was to survive, both of us had to go all in on fundraising. Fundraising became our number-one priority. Having a good partnership helps if you're trying to go long on your idea. It's just too much for one person.

## Fundraising in a Pandemic

Then the coronavirus happened. Well, 2020 happened. Between the pandemic, the economic collapse, the California wildfires, and the death of Sean Connery, is there anything 2020 didn't ruin? In the future, when your meal at a restaurant or your rental car is just terrible, we're betting you'll tell your friends, "It was so 2020." It will become the ultimate insult. That's how bad that year was.

But we digress. When news of the virus first came out of China in January 2020, most people weren't that concerned. It seemed unlikely that the disease would come to our shores. However, by early February, more cases were beginning to appear, and the financial markets were becoming deeply concerned. On March 9, 2020, the S&P 500 dropped 7 percent in the first four minutes after the exchange opened, which triggered a "circuit breaker" that stopped trading for fifteen minutes—the first time that had happened since the financial crisis in 2007.

In the financial world, there's an old saying: "When the US sneezes, the entire world catches a cold." Ironic but also accurate: as it became clear to global investors what the pandemic meant for the economy, markets around the world started getting very nervous. Losses mounted, and jobs and businesses began disappearing. We were concerned about our ability to close funding for Mynd, but we also thought that, as in 2008, crisis might bring opportunity. The financial world seemed to concur, as a passage from this *PitchBook* analyst note from March 2020 illustrates:

> Today, it seems that virtually every VC remains "open for business," but deal terms appear to have shifted in favor of investors as startups do whatever they can to close on capital. This could be a catalyst for a shift from the prevailing market in recent years, which has been categorized by a broad-based shift toward founder-friendly terms and ever-higher valuations. Startups do have a variety of options outside of traditional VC, but the viability of most of those options in a downturn has yet to be tested.

We had been hearing the same things throughout the private equity and venture capital worlds for months. Yes, things were scary and uncertain, but they were sitting on cash to invest. If we could get in front of the right people, we could land our C round. And since we were once again down to a few months' worth of capital to run Mynd, we really had no choice.

Between the chicanery of WeWork and the prospect of a global economic shutdown, investors were seriously spooked. And as you know, when investors get nervous, they are no different than consumers: they stop spending and start stuffing money into their mattresses. Most of the investors we met with snapped their checkbooks shut without really looking at the opportunity in front of them. But we saw it. If the economy shut down, millions of people would be spending most of their waking hours at home. More than ever, landlords and property managers would need effective ways to communicate with their renters. We knew that when the dust settled, proptech would be even hotter than it had been before. We just needed someone who saw what we saw.

## Staying Afloat in Rough Waters

By February 2020, the constant rejection had rubbed us raw. It's tough psychologically because you start to wonder if what you're seeing is just a mirage. If you think about *The Big Short*, that's exactly the same dynamic those early short sellers experienced when the bond ratings agencies and the investment banks refused to downgrade the mortgage bonds that were propping up the economy, even though millions of defaults had rendered them worthless. They started wondering if they had been wrong despite the reams of data telling them they were right. By spring 2020, we knew how they felt. It was hard to stay positive.

There were also some empirical reasons for the rejections. Our gross margins were too low for many investors' comfort. Also, our lifetime value to customer acquisition cost ratio was too low, meaning investors were uncomfortable with what it was costing us to acquire new customers versus the lifetime value we expected to get from those customers. In other words, we didn't yet have enough traction on direct sales. Meanwhile, we figured we had enough cash to keep the doors open until June, so we had to find someone who believed in our business—and do it quickly.

During this time, we learned another important lesson about going long: *it never happens the same way twice.* When we decided to think big with Waypoint, the only thing between us and an unprecedented opportunity was capital. When we were able to secure sufficient funds, we were able to grow as fast as our system and our people would let us. We couldn't have known Mynd would be different when we started it, but by 2020, it was clear that this big long play would come with its own challenges that we had never experienced before.

For example, after we finally closed our C round, when it had become clear that COVID-19 might become a serious brake on growth, we had to come back to our new investors with a new budget and plan. Like every other company in every sector of the economy, we were adapting in real time to an unprecedented situation.

## Wells Fargo Returns

Remember back in the Introduction when we told you about trying to raise our first big round of capital and debt and that we'd had a debt deal with Wells Fargo sewn up, only for them to cancel the deal at the eleventh hour? We shared that with you because, ironically, in 2020, Wells Fargo stepped up and led our C round.

We kept pushing through the rejection and fear (and our own discouragement), and by February, we had started to build a round. We had a setback with one terrific VC that we had hoped would lead our syndicate. It turned out that one of its investors was problematic for other investors. When some of our other possible investors saw that, they backed out. If we were going to keep this VC on board, they couldn't be our lead.

Then Wells Fargo contacted us and said, "We would be willing to lead." This was huge because Wells Fargo has a strong institutional brand. We went back to the other VC and said, "We love you guys, but this is a real problem for us. Would you mind not leading?" That meant they would forfeit a seat on the Mynd board, but to their tremendous credit and our tremendous relief, they agreed. This VC really took the high road and was a great team player and partner.

Like having an A-list actor at the top of the cast list can help a movie, having Wells Fargo at the top of our ticket helped us. Our other investors were supportive of the change, so now we had to build out the rest of the syndicate and bring in other investors. Finally, a large pension fund came in at the eleventh hour and invested $15 million of the $41.5 million we ended up raising. That was critical. We would not have been comfortable closing at just $25 million. That wouldn't have given us enough runway to grow. If that pension fund hadn't joined, we might not have gotten the deal closed.

It was the ultimate Hail Mary. When you hear other people's start-up stories and you hear about how they were told no one hundred times or more, it's hard not to extrapolate all those "No" answers into the probability of your own situation and conclude, "Why bother?" The answer is, because you never know what's around the corner. This pension fund came out of nowhere, and after they did, we could barely believe it. We'd had so many false positives, and now we had a major investor that seemed genuinely excited.

Doug said, "I have a feeling about this one. This could be the one that pushes us over the edge." Of course, you never know until the deal closes. The pension fund was the investor we were the most nervous about changing its mind during COVID-19 because we had the newest relationship. Now we had a syndicate of seven. If we could hold it together until closing, Mynd would have the capital it needed. Meanwhile, there was no plan B. There was no viable scenario for saving the company if we didn't raise this round. If we had been forced to shut down, we probably would have held a fire sale.

It was a tough time psychologically. There was a concern that anyone might pull out. Technically we could have closed at a lower amount, but everybody knew we needed $40 million to be viable, and it makes the deal riskier if you don't have enough capital to support the plan everybody was investing in. Any of our investors pulling out could have created a cascading problem, like a run on a bank. Our board members were calling us every day—sometimes multiple times a day—demanding to know what was going on and wondering if we were going to get this deal closed. Meanwhile, we were trying not to show our cards to our Mynd team so they wouldn't panic. All the while, we knew the company would fail if we didn't get this money. It was like having five fires burning at the same time. It was a test of patience and nerve.

Finally, against all odds, in the third week in February, we had a signed term sheet. As COVID-19 got worse throughout March, we maintained contact with our investors every day. We had to keep them calm while not letting them see that we were panicked.

It's a real testament to our investors that they all stuck with the deal. We closed on April 2. Just three weeks earlier, on March 11, three extraordinary things had happened: the NBA suspended its season after Utah Jazz player Rudy Gobert tested positive, incoming flights from Europe were canceled, and the longest bull market in the history of the US stock market came to an end. That was quite the backdrop for our deal closing. The whole world seemed to be falling apart, but now our world was going to spin on a while longer.

We delayed announcing the news until after the spring 2020 COVID-19 emergency calmed down a little. Finally, on June 29, 2020, the following finally ran on *Business Wire*:

> Oakland, Calif.—Mynd Property Management, a full-stack tech-enabled property management company scaling the non-institutional segment of the $20-billion-plus single-family rental (SFR) sector, closed a Series C round of financing totaling $41.5 million. Wells Fargo led the round, joined by Mynd's existing Silicon Valley investors, Canaan Partners, Lightspeed Venture Partners, and Jackson Square Ventures.
>
> With more than 7,500 homes under management in 16 markets and expanding, Mynd is one of the largest SFR property management firms in the U.S. By investing in disruptive technology, the company has unlocked the potential of virtual property management.

We'd managed to catch lightning in a bottle for a second time. The relief and gratitude were overwhelming.

## Never Let a Good Crisis Go to Waste

We're thrilled that we were able to pull off our C round for a lot of reasons, but one of them is that the experience offered us a chance to reinvent ourselves for a second time. The desire to do that has taken root throughout the company. We feel more confident than ever about our future, and part of the reason is the new perspective this experience gave us.

Initially with Mynd, we were on this breakneck growth cycle, trying to double in size every year. Now we're saying we need to kind of hunker down and stretch out our cash, because growth is expensive and our board felt that we needed to conserve cash. Part of our strategy to conserve cash was to cease all M&A activity. In 2019, the year before, a meaningful portion of our growth came from M&A, so this was a big shift for us.

Instead, we're going to really focus on our business processes, our technology, and our organizational structure, simplifying everything throughout the business and making it better. We've also used the opportunity to get rid of a lot of our old customers who were with us before we found the right product market fit. Now we're fully focusing on single-family rentals. Those calls would have been hard to make if we had been holding ourselves to a growth pace of doubling every year. But instead, we were saying, "Let's stretch our capital out. Let's not grow much in 2020 during COVID-19 until we know more about what the world looks like. Let's cull our portfolio of all those bad units and replace them with new ones."

It was a relatively slow-growth strategy but sustainable: grow slowly but steadily in 2020, then hit the gas to grow aggressively in 2021 and beyond. That's exactly what we've done.

There's a famous Winston Churchill quote that goes, "Never

let a good crisis go to waste." We've listened . . . twice. Because we did, we've been fortunate enough to be present at the birth of an industry. Rich Ford, an investment banker at Jefferies, was the first investment banker to focus on SFR, and he organized the first conference geared toward single-family rental as an industry. Colin spoke at that conference in 2012 with some of the early players like American Homes 4 Rent. There were maybe two hundred people in a back room at the Fairview Park Marriott in Washington, DC, and the consensus was that we were all fighting the same battles, dealing with government scrutiny, and we needed a trade association. During that event, a lot of people came up to Colin and said, "You and Doug launched this entire industry."

There are a lot of other people who shared in creating this industry, but it certainly feels good to be considered among its leaders. Now, there's even an industry trade group called the National Rental Home Council, and every major player in the industry is a member, including Mynd.

## Where We Are and What We Know

Today Mynd has more than three hundred and fifty employees, and we're thriving. When COVID-19 hit, we moved our people to remote work, and that's gone very well. In fact, it's going so well that if we hadn't just signed a five-year lease on our office, we'd consider becoming a totally virtual company. We already were a sort of hybrid remote company because most of our engineers are in Eastern Europe and Russia. Since day one, we've had engineers around the world working in high-definition video in our conference rooms and using Google Meet. Using tools like Slack was always part of our culture.

Everything was set up for remote work from day one. If you decided you didn't want to go into work one day or your kid had a doctor's appointment, you could still attend all your meetings on the computer. Everybody's as productive as they ever were, and probably more so, because a lot of our people like working from home. So Mynd will probably always be a part office, part remote company. It makes sense; we're a tech platform, after all. Allowing people to work from home also improves our ability to hire the best, because now our recruitment area can be anywhere in the world there's reliable Wi-Fi.

What have we learned through all this? Lots of things. For one thing, if you want to go long on your idea, you can't do it halfway. You have to jump out of the plane and hope you have a parachute on your back. You need *audacity*. Waypoint was audacious, buying up houses at the nadir of an economic collapse when everyone else thought SFR was a dead end. Mynd's start was just as bold—building the technology, hiring the teams, and putting together a full-service platform when no one else was doing it.

Many entrepreneurs would advise you to slow-play your hand, to test your concept to make sure the demand is there. You can do that, but you risk someone else overtaking you. When you go big, go big. With Mynd, we felt like we had enough insight into the players and the market to say, "Let's do this and get out ahead of everyone else." Remember sailboat racing? It's the same idea. We knew the software was the bottleneck to scaling the SFR management business, so our solution was to build the software ourselves.

We can't declare victory yet, but we're definitely in "go big or go home" mode with Mynd. For better or worse, the one who gets out there first takes all the risks but can also catch the best wind.

It's hard, but if you get out there first and you're successful, you have a better chance to create something really special.

## Prioritized Focus

Another thing we've learned about going long on an idea is that you have to prioritize focus. Taking an idea from nothing to something will pull you in a hundred directions, but you can't do everything at once. You have to know where to focus your time and attention and reduce distractions. Being an entrepreneur is like swatting mosquitoes in the Everglades: for every bug that gets your attention, there are twenty more that will drive you crazy. In business, distractions are endless and constant. If you're not hiring or raising capital, you're talking to the press, working hard on the next prototype of your product, working on your pitch, responding to emails, or sitting in endless meetings. That's not even accounting for the technical, legal, financial, and personnel fires you have to put out. It's amazing that anything gets done.

That is why from the beginning of Waypoint, we've placed an emphasis on focus. We don't get distracted. We're good at getting up every day and saying, "What needs to get done today? Let's do that." Entrepreneurs have to remain focused and learn to delegate or let things go, because when you're the face of your company and the chief architect of its vision, you're going to be pulled in a hundred directions at once. If you can't focus, you'll drown.

The key is *prioritized focus*. With a start-up, every day brings another life-and-death matter. At the same time, there will be twenty other matters that *seem* like life-and-death. It's your job to push aside the lesser priorities and drill down to the one priority that's important at that moment. Figure out what matters most, and put your mind and energy there. Get it done and then move on.

Doug's great at prioritizing focus. The proof is in his career as an NFL placekicker because you don't last in that job without an incredible ability to block out distractions. Imagine . . . it's the fourth quarter, you're standing forty-five yards away from the goal, there are three seconds on the clock, and the game is tied. Seventy thousand fans are screaming, eleven human tanks averaging about three hundred pounds are waiting to crush you into the grass, and whether your team wins or loses depends on what you do with your right leg. If you're going to put that ball through the uprights, you need a level of focus that's almost inhuman.

We had to bring that kind of focus not only to Waypoint but to closing our C round with Mynd when we were trying to keep our investors cool even as the world seemed to be coming apart. Prioritized focus is the answer. It keeps you from being overwhelmed. You don't have to limit yourself to one goal or task in a day; you can set your priorities in any way you like. Give yourself a time limit. Focus on one job until it's finished. Prioritize by the time of day. Do what works for you. You don't just become more productive. You control the chaos.

Being an entrepreneur is like standing on the deck of a ship in heavy weather. It's hard to find your footing, and you have to constantly shift your balance to stay on your feet. By setting and resetting your priorities, you become comfortable with surrendering control and with disorder—two constants for any entrepreneur. You also lower your chances of burnout because you're not spending everything you've got on one task until you have nothing left. You stay more alert and more capable of leading.

We've also learned that if you're going to be an entrepreneur, it's incredibly valuable to find a counterpart whose skills and attitude complement yours and to work as a team. We can't imagine doing it any other way. We constantly bounce ideas off each other. If one of us says, "I've been focused on such-and-such all day," and the other questions it, we know to stop for a second and ask, "Where should our focus be? Is this the best use of our time?" That lets us reboot, choose a fresh priority for the next day (or three hours or ninety minutes), and it's ready, set, go.

We've also had to learn to let things go, and that's valuable because entrepreneurs can be obsessive. You might feel like you have to do everything yourself in order for it to be done right. But when you're forced to delegate and trust your colleagues or employees to get the job done, you can relax (assuming that you've hired great people). You can say to yourself, "I'm not the only one around here with game. Good to know." After a while, you stop feeling like the world is resting on your shoulders. That's a good feeling.

Finally, we've learned that the only way to survive as an entrepreneur in this world is to be true to what you care about. We've done what makes us happy and stuck to our values, come what may. We're entrepreneurs, which means we love creating new things, taking on challenges, and making our own rules. Neither of us has ever been interested in "having a job." If you're enjoying yourself and doing something you love with great people, you might be working long hours, but you'll feel great, like you do after an exhilarating workout.

It's easiest to do that when your professional life reflects who you are. We see lots of entrepreneurs trying to live up to the stereotype of the Silicon Valley player—living large, talking fast, trying to change the world—when that's not their strength. If your business doesn't reflect what you care about, it won't be sustainable. If it does, you will work harder and better and attract people who will match you passion for passion.

For instance, in our post-Waypoint lives, we've become big on education. The way we see it, the more you learn and the more successes you have, the more you have a responsibility to share what you know with others. We both love teaching, so we teach business courses at Stanford and Cal for the joy of sharing what we've learned with others. We've learned many valuable lessons in business, and it's rewarding to share them with other entrepreneurs, especially young entrepreneurs. Sharing experiences—what happened, why it happened, and how we responded—is a much more effective way to help someone than telling them, "Do this." We also learn at least as much as we teach.

In building Waypoint, and again in building Mynd, we've never forgotten who we are: two regular guys with a little bit of talent and a lot of nerve, willing to go long on something we believed in. There's not much more to our formula than that. If it works for you, that's terrific.

Would we do it a third time? Sell Mynd or take it public, leave with big golden parachutes, and then turn around and start Company Number Three? Hard to say, but probably not. Starting a company is exciting, but it's also exhausting. We've done it together twice now, and we're probably going to look for different ways to do entrepreneurial things in the future. For example, we have a company that invests in start-ups, and that's enjoyable. We love doing the detective work to find promising small companies whose founders have gumption and vision, fund them, and then work with them to a successful launch. But we probably won't want to run them.

Starting companies is like having a baby. Talk to any woman who's given birth more than once, and she'll probably tell you that the first pregnancy was rough and giving birth was painful. After some time passed, she forgot about the pain and wanted another baby. Then when that pregnancy and birth were more difficult than the first, she was done. She probably looked at her husband and told him a vasectomy would make a wonderful anniversary present.

We've had our second baby, and both have come at great cost. With Waypoint, there was the incredible stress of the FBI investigation and the constant pressure to raise capital. There was the stress of going public and then being less happy in a company that we didn't recognize anymore. We've learned that part of being a smart entrepreneur is knowing when to throw in the towel and do something else. We could see ourselves buying properties purely as buy-and-hold investments and being advisors to start-ups. Otherwise, we're interested in enjoying the payoff of all our work. There comes a point where the grind of starting a traditional company with an IPO in your sights becomes too much.

Waypoint was a great learning experience that validated our original hypothesis, but Mynd is the play of a lifetime—and we use the word *play* on purpose. This is still great fun for us. We're having a blast. When it stops being fun, we'll walk away. Any entrepreneur should be prepared to do that.

# CHAPTER TEN

# Predict the Future

Of course, Mynd is evolving. We're evolving in our outlook on business and what we want to do next. That's essential, because if you want to go long on something, you need to perceive the opportunity before most of the market knows what's happening. The world is unpredictable. Take residential real estate. With the economic devastation caused by COVID-19, you might have expected housing prices to drop. Nope. As we're writing this in the spring of 2021, SFR is booming like never before. Housing prices are up across the vast majority of markets in the US. Four and a half years into our journey with Mynd, and we're in the middle of the biggest inundation of capital and demand in the history of SFR. As we see it, we're about to catch another major tailwind that's going to blow up the market for years to come.

So let's put on our futurist hats for a few minutes and talk about trends and the future. After all, the future's where we're all going to be living, right?

First things first. How did home prices skyrocket when so many people were hurting economically? Well, home prices are driven by the simple law of supply and demand. The foreclosure crisis of 2008 was caused in part by vast overbuilding, which was indirectly caused by loose lending practices. That led to a building boom of about 1.5 million new homes being built per year from 1999 to 2007, peaking at about two million in 2006.

Then came the financial meltdown and the resulting crash in home prices, and everyone overcompensated. After a fifty-year average of about 1.4 million new homes per year, the period from 2009 to 2014 saw the lowest rate of building in half a century, with an average of just 720,000 new homes annually. When people began buying homes again as the crisis lifted, this construction shortfall led to an extreme undersupply of homes that continues to this day. The excess inventory built from 2005 to 2008 has been absorbed, and in most major markets, there simply are not enough homes for all the people who want to buy them, which leads to bidding wars and skyrocketing prices.

Even now, in 2021, with the rate of building creeping back up, we're still not at the level we need to maintain a steady balance between supply and demand—about 1.5 million new homes per year. It's still a seller's market. So even though home prices have been going up for a long time, we're optimistic that they will continue going up.

That would have happened even without the COVID-19 pandemic, but by changing how we live, the pandemic has also changed the real estate market. Urban cores are becoming ghost towns, not just for residential real estate but also commercial real estate as companies realize they don't need huge office suites when they can have half their workforces working from home. Meanwhile, vacation markets like Lake Tahoe are through the roof. So is suburbia.

When lockdowns came in 2020, many people decided that if they had to shelter in place for months, they would rather do it in a single-family home in the suburbs where they had more space and a yard, not a tiny fourth-floor walk-up in Manhattan. If you look at SFR as an asset class, it's typically located in the suburbs and is better for renters at the higher socioeconomic levels who have not been hit by the type of unemployment we saw with COVID-19.

That's why when you look at metrics like rent growth, occupancy rates, and delinquency rates, single-family rentals are blowing the doors off of multifamily rentals. Now that there's a decade-long track record of companies like Waypoint and Mynd thriving in this space and multiple public SFR companies that have been performing well in the markets for five-plus years, we're finally seeing unprecedented institutional capital flooding into the US housing industry—from asset managers who are managing funds of a trillion dollars or more.

Because of that, one of the things we're predicting is that institutional investors, who own over 50 percent of multifamily rentals right now but own only about 2 percent of SFRs, will buy as many as three to four hundred thousand SFR homes per year over the next five years. That is a trend that is just now beginning. SFR has become a legitimate, sought-after asset class, just as we always thought it could be.

At Mynd, we're part of that. The way we're set up as a platform in control of our own technology, with a nimble operating model, we are very well positioned to take a disproportionate share of that incoming capital flowing into this space. In fact, in addition to managing properties, we are ramping up a buying operation. We will buy on behalf of large institutions and then manage construction and maintenance. It's coming full circle back to Waypoint but with a different structure and a better tech stack.

There's something else at work too. As of March 2021, when the $1.9 trillion stimulus package was signed into law, more money has been printed in the last two years than at any time in history. The monetary supply increased by 25 percent in 2020, and that was before the Biden stimulus. That relates to inflation. But inflation isn't the right thing to be looking at. Inflation is based on a basket of goods—the consumer price index, gasoline prices, and things like that—that aren't relevant here. For our discussion, what matters is the price of assets. In the context of home price appreciation, a home is an asset like gold, Bitcoin, or a stock. In general, assets go up in value proportionally to the money supply, which is why with this historically unprecedented printing of money, the value of all of these assets is going through the roof simultaneously. There are reasons to think there will be more stimulus coming, which means the government will be printing more money. That will continue to increase the monetary supply, which will increase the prices of assets.

All this change will probably play out over at least a decade. SFR is such a vast untapped market, and institutional investors are just discovering it and figuring out how to innovate within it, so it will take at least that long for the inflow of capital to have a disruptive impact. But it will happen. SFR performs well and has performed consistently. It's a way for big investors to be in a different asset class and increase the diversification of their real estate portfolios.

## Accelerating Innovation

Proptech is experiencing the same kind of exponential growth curve as SFR. COVID-19 has been an accelerant for digitizing an industry that has been way behind the curve. From office space to residential, people have become more comfortable interfacing in a digital environment because they've had to. The real estate industry has lagged behind most other industries in adopting technology as a way to do business. (Health care is another.)

When COVID-19 hit and people had to change everything about an industry that had been conducted on an on-location, face-to-face basis, there was a great deal of pent-up demand for the solutions we're seeing. In real estate, a lot of people made a lot of money by doing the same thing the same way again and again. When you add the fact that the cycle time in real estate development is long, it's an industry that hasn't seen a lot of change. Even though there was a need for greater efficiencies and economies of scale, the sector sat in a technology vacuum until technologies like mobile, cloud, and AI became more powerful, widely available, and cost effective. Then the dam burst.

Waypoint and Mynd rode the early part of that wave in the SFR space, but proptech was already changing things in other sectors. Probably the first game changer in proptech was Zillow, the grandfather of them all, founded in 2004. They've completely changed expectations of how home buyers, sellers, and real estate agents interact with listings and each other. Before Zillow, the idea of buying a house without doing a walk-through was unthinkable; now, in red-hot residential markets, buyers will tour a house virtually on Opendoor and make an offer to get ahead of the competition.

Probably the most successful proptech company is Airbnb,

founded in 2008. They've disrupted not only the residential short-term rental space but hospitality, as well, while creating a whole new economy of landlords who own and manage vacation rentals through their platform. As of this writing, they have a market cap of about $113 billion.

The real estate space is hungry for innovation, so in proptech, innovation is everywhere. A young company called Pacaso is changing the second home market with co-ownership of vacation homes in locations like Napa and Palm Springs. They're an absolute rocket ship because they make it relatively affordable to own one-eighth of a fantastic vacation home without any of the hassles. They will be an Airbnb, a household name, in five to ten years.

The pandemic has sparked a huge wave of innovations. While homeowners were in lockdown, they were understandably uncomfortable with the idea of a repairman coming into their homes to fix a broken washer or water heater. No problem. Companies like Fixer and ResHub (a new telemaintenance company started by our former Waypoint colleague Mike Travalini) can resolve repair and maintenance issues virtually. Instead of having a technician come to your home, these companies either give you an app packed with DIY instructions or connect you via video-conference with a professional technician who can diagnose the issue and walk you through the repair. If someone does need to come to your home, they've gathered enough information that they can be in and out fast.

Before COVID-19, you couldn't give that kind of service away. People either had repairmen come to their home or conducted research to learn how to do the repair themselves. Now they love the virtual support and guidance they receive. It's like telemedicine—the need to be socially distant has changed our thinking on what kind of interaction is necessary to complete a transaction and get quality service.

Now there are venture capitalists who focus just on the proptech space, like Fifth Wall, which has about $1 billion under management across three funds. Clelia Peters, one of the founding members of a New York incubator called MetaProp, is on the Mynd board, and she's credited with coining the term *proptech*. We asked her about that and this fast-changing sector of the economy that she's watched from the beginning of its evolution.

"My father was involved in the real estate industry, and my partner, his father was involved in the real estate industry," Clelia says. "Some senior people in the New York City real estate world agreed to meet with us to talk about our excitement about real estate tech. Mostly, the way those meetings went was that we'd sit down and talk to them about the wave of innovation that was about to come into this space. We'd tell them, 'Proptech is going to be the new fintech. The way we do everything from dirt to disposition is going to change.' They would basically listen to us, a little bit bored, and then say, 'Thanks for coming in, guys.'

"That was 2014," Clelia continues. "Over the course of the following twelve months, there was starting to be a shift. We started to get inbound calls from people saying, 'I hear about this happening, I hear about that happening.' There's been an enormous acceleration since that time. I don't think there was a single major real estate company that had a dedicated person focused on technology or innovation. It was not seen as a core strategic issue…in part because a component of real estate just hasn't been broken.

"There's a lot of inefficiency in the way that we manage buildings, but LPs build that inefficiency into what they expect in terms of returns," she goes on. "So people who managed real estate assets felt like they weren't under any pressure to deliver something different. A lot of the experimentation around innovation in the early days came primarily from family businesses that were not answerable to someone else but were thinking, 'How do we increase value?'"

And the origin story of the term "proptech"? Clelia cleared that one up for us. "When we first started talking about this, we called it 'retech,'" she concludes. "There was some dude who had bought the domain retech.com, and he had a blog where he wrote about the intersection of real estate and technology. We started talking about retech, and this guy sent us a cease and desist letter. So we were like, 'What do we call this?' Well, in Europe, they call the real estate market the property market, and in Europe, sometimes they refer to the technology as proptech. So we adopted the term proptech, and that became the broadly used term in the United States. Ultimately, I think the term transferred back to Europe, and it became the dominant term there as well.

"But at the time, we thought retech was better, and we were really bummed."

## Innovation and Disruption

Whatever you call it, the reality is that technology is changing virtually everything about how we interact with real estate—not just in terms of how we buy, manage, and invest in properties but how we live in them. For example, since COVID-19, mobility has become incredibly important to people. In our parents' and grandparents' generation, people might have one job for their whole careers. They would work for General Motors for forty years and then retire. Now the average person might hold more than ten jobs over the course of their career, and with remote work becoming so important and so widely accepted, mobility has become more important than ever. As a result, renting versus owning a home makes more sense than ever for millions.

Studies have shown that if you own a house, you're much less likely to move somewhere else for a job. That lack of mobility really impedes people's career growth, even more so now that there's this ability to be a digital nomad and work from anywhere. People, especially if they're young and single, don't necessarily care about putting down roots as much as they once did. Rather they value being able to work where they want and live the lifestyle they want, and renting fits those goals a lot better than owning.

That's led to all kinds of innovations, and not just Airbnb. Now we have different rent-to-own structures, different equity and debt structures. There's an astonishing amount of innovation, driven by technology and data, that's allowing people to live in homes with all kinds of alternative financing arrangements that no one had even considered three to five years ago.

We asked our friend and colleague Aaron Edelheit, former CEO of American Home and current CEO of Mindset Capital, for some other examples, and he gave us some. "You're going to see penetration of these technologies in everything from the way properties are built, the way properties are inspected, and the way properties are maintained," Aaron says. "I was one of the first investors in this company called Flow Technology that made automatic water shutoff systems that can detect leaks as small as a drop per minute and shut off the water. There's going to be wave upon wave of what I'll call 'preventive maintenance technology' around properties that will change the way that properties are run and managed.

"It comes at the exact point at which we're having a pretty dramatic shortage in skilled labor," he continues. "You know, the average age of a plumber is fifty-six, and I've seen estimates that in the next five years, 25 percent of all plumbers will retire. I don't know about you, but very few people actually know how the plumbing in their house works, and it's not a skill that you can easily do by yourself. This is just one example of how proptech can step in and help alleviate a crisis.

"Insurance is going to be disrupted too," Aaron concludes. "Take a look at a company like Hippo; I wouldn't want to compete with them. When you sign up, they not only make it easy using technology, but they'll send you a bunch of preventive information on ways to protect your home. They're thinking about things in a very different way."

Proptech even extends to how homes are built. The other part of the supply and demand crisis in housing is the cost of labor and construction. We're involved with a company called Plant Prefab that's leading the field of modular homebuilding. Now more homes than ever are prebuilt in factories and shipped as near-complete modules to the building site, where contractors can assemble them in a tiny fraction of the time of traditional homebuilding. We're not talking about ugly industrial buildings or mobile homes either but beautiful, state-of-the-art homes that wouldn't be out of place in a high-end neighborhood. Faster, cheaper, more efficient construction means lower building costs and more homes finished in less time.

## Democratizing Wealth Creation

In the coming years, it's clear to us that there will be no limit to the innovative thinking around real estate, often powered by technology. Some real estate companies are leveraging data and technology to figure out the perfect size and price per square foot to optimize demand. Others are pushing the boundaries with new financial models, such as joint ventures with property owners that enable the owner to get some revenue out of land that they're not using without bearing any of the up-front expense. Modular construction will compress the time it takes to build new projects and help companies develop new, creative ways to build at high density.

Housing affordability is also a huge issue, and there are now coliving companies like PadSplit (which we're involved with) whose whole business model is to take a house and convert as many rooms into bedrooms as the local building codes will allow. They use a different mousetrap to bring in folks who are paying $200 or $300 per month for a furnished bedroom. These are membership arrangements, and these companies deal with the organizational challenges of having six or seven different people living in a house by establishing rules and a membership culture. But what they're really doing is making it so people making minimum wage can live in a single-family home. It's a new model that's working. PadSplit is a cool company, and it's really taking off.

If we had to make predictions about the future, there are a few developments we're confident about. First, institutional ownership of SFR will become commensurate with institutional ownership of multifamily. That means millions of units becoming institutionally owned. People get nervous about that, but at the end of the day, apartments used to be a very mom-and-pop asset class. But when institutions started investing, the level of professionalism and the experience became much better. Yes, in certain places, prices went up, but that was driven by supply and demand.

People will have more choices. Real estate is a white canvas that hasn't been painted on yet. That's why you're seeing so much innovation in everything from smart locks to whole houses tied together with data and technology. Within twenty years, almost every new residential structure is going to be built, component by component, in a manufacturing warehouse, and a lot of those will be 3D printed. It's already happening. The construction is higher quality, more environmentally friendly, and a lot faster.

In the end, our mission is really to democratize investment and wealth creation—to make it possible for more people to participate. Technology is making that possible too. The reason a lot of younger, less wealthy people don't invest in real estate is because it's hard. It's this disconnected, intimidating ecosystem. It's complicated to find the right market, find the right asset, figure out how to finance and insure it, and manage the property. One solution comes from simple, app-based companies like Fundrise, which allow inexperienced investors to invest in a low-cost, diversified portfolio of institutional-quality real estate.

Our Mynd investment platform is another. As we get ready to raise our Series D, we are creating a twenty-first century investment platform with all the services and data that a retail investor needs to be successful within one system. We're democratizing real estate, reducing friction. We have all the data and can pick the best markets. We'll help people buy, finance, and manage their properties with the power of all that data in one system and make life better for the tenants as well.

As we evolve, we'll use our data to create even greater value for people. For example, we can make it easier for someone who lives in the Bay Area to buy a house in Houston so they can get a little piece of equity that they otherwise never would have gotten. Wealth creation happens through equity. It's not W2 income; that's too heavily taxed. The scales are heavily tilted toward equity, and who gets to own equity? People who own real estate. For people who might have avoided real estate investing because they saw it as too complex, intimidating, or costly, we're working to make it much easier to build wealth through equity.

As we were putting the final touches on this book, we closed one of the largest deals in the history of SFR with Invesco, a multi-trillion dollar global asset manager. This deal will transform the SFR industry once again. Invesco is making a $5 billion commitment to buy SFR homes through Mynd, a move that will steer us back toward a business model with strong similarities to Waypoint, albeit with a new fee-for-services model.

In this partnership, we will apply all of the knowhow we gained in growing Waypoint to build a full-stack buying and construction management platform, enabling Invesco to buy as many as twenty thousand homes. This is game-changing. By going all-in on SFR, Invesco—one of the world's largest true commercial real estate investors—has signaled its arrival as a legitimate, desirable commercial real estate asset class. They wouldn't invest in SFR if it weren't fully vetted and accepted and if their worldwide pension and endowment fund investors didn't want SFR.

In a way, we've come full circle.

What began for us in 2008 as a "big long" venture to leverage an opportunity nobody else could see has become a mission to help bridge the gap between the haves and the have-nots—to help the have-nots tap into the greatest wealth-creation vehicle known to capitalism. In the last two hundred years, 90 percent of millionaires have said that real estate was a meaningful contributor to their wealth creation.

That power shouldn't be restricted to a privileged few. It should be available to anyone with the moxie and intelligence to see the potential of real estate and technology and a few dollars to invest. Making that possible is the epitome of big long thinking. If there's anything you take away from this book, it's that thinking big and going long is always the way to build something extraordinary.

# Acknowledgments

The Waypoint journey was both terrifying and exhilarating. As a team, we did things that we never thought possible. We want to thank the amazing Waypoint team for all of your exhaustive efforts, extremely hard work, and sleepless nights you put into the company. We would have never had any of the success we had without you all. We hope you enjoyed the ride as much as we did.

To the Mynd Team, which includes many former Waypointers: we are thrilled to be boarding another rocket ship to see if we can take things further than we ever did at Waypoint. We appreciate all of your efforts. We have come a long way toward building out our vision in just over five years. Onward!

To our friends and mentors who helped us along the way: we had no playbook, and neither of us had any real experience in scaling a business. We are forever grateful for all of the love, support, advice, counseling, and encouragement you shared with us. We are exceptionally thankful for having you in our lives and allowing us to create great memories.

We would especially like to thank our families, who supported us throughout the entire Waypoint journey and the writing of this book. We really needed your support!

A very special thank-you to those who took time out of their busy schedules to be involved with us bringing our story to life:

- Joe Maehler
- Charles Young
- Nina Tran
- Rich Rodriquez
- Ali Nazar
- David Zanaty

The last thirteen-plus years in the single family rental industry have been a blast. We look forward to making history with all of you again!